TWENTIETH CENTURY WOMEN OF ACHIEVEMENT

TWENTIETH CENTURY WOMEN OF ACHIEVEMENT

Samuel Kostman

cop, a

RICHARDS ROSEN PRESS, INC.

New York, New York 10010

Published in 1976 by Richards Rosen Press, Inc.
29 East 21st Street, New York, N.Y. 10010

FIRST EDITION
Second Printing

Manufactured in the United States of America

Library of Congress Cataloging in Publication Data

Kostman, Samuel.
   Twentieth century women of achievement.

   (MS series)
   Includes bibliographies.
   CONTENTS: Mary Baker Eddy.—Mary McLeod Bethune.
—Margaret Sanger. [etc.]
   1. Women—Biography. [1. Biography] I. Title.
HQ1154.K665   920.72 [920]   75–31557
ISBN 0–8239–0333–8

To my wife Ruth
Companion and inspiration

About the Author

Samuel Kostman is principal of George Washington High School, a post which is considered by many the most challenging educational administrator's position in New York City. During his five years at this embattled school, Mr. Kostman has introduced educational innovations such as George Washington Prep, a nationally acclaimed alternative school, the Four Day Week Program, independent study projects and an expanded English as a Second Language program.

Earlier in his career Mr. Kostman was chairman of the English Department at Wingate High School in Brooklyn. He also taught English and Hebrew at Midwood High School in Brooklyn and Isidore and Ida Straus Jr. H.S. in the Brownsville-East New York area. Mr. Kostman was a Talmud Torah teacher for seventeen years and served in resident camps for almost twenty-five years as a counselor, group leader, head counselor and camp director. For several years he worked as a youth leader and assistant program director for the Young Israel of Boro Park in Brooklyn.

His professional associations include membership in many

local and national organizations and committees. At present he is a member of the Executive Board of the High School Principal's Association of New York City and was a member of the Special Executive Development Training Program of the Board of Education in conjunction with Automation House. Mr. Kostman serves as an assistant examiner for the Board of Education, as a member of the City-Wide Committee on Introducing More Paperback Books onto the New York State Textbook List and the Board of Education's Language Arts Textbook Evaluation Committee. He has taught in-service teacher training and assistant principal workshops and has created many new courses and materials in the area of high school language arts. He also served on the committees which eventually drafted the courses of study for junior and senior high school Hebrew courses in the public schools. Mr. Kostman also serves as the editor for Barron's English Regents Examination answer booklets.

In private life Mr. Kostman is active in civic and communal affairs. He is presently serving on the Board of Education of the Yeshiva of Flatbush and Solomon Schecter High School in Brooklyn and is active in Mizrachi, Israel Bond drives, the struggle for Soviet Jewry and the Jewish National Fund.

Acknowledgments

The author is deeply indebted to his wife Ruth for typing the manuscript and for her creative services as critic and editor. He is also grateful to his children Gail, Joy and Ira for their comments, suggestions and patience.

Mrs. Helen Margalith, librarian-in-charge at George Washington High School, has also earned the author's gratitude for her unlimited helpfulness and patience during the year that he worked on the book. She provided much of the research material.

While their contributions were instrumental in providing this work with much of its substance and quality, the author assumes full responsibility for whatever errors or shortcomings it may have.

Contents

Introduction

It was Oscar Wilde, the famous English man of letters, who once said of women that they are "creatures meant to be loved, not to be understood." In that aphorism are imbedded many of the prejudices that men have had against women through the ages. They often believed members of the female sex are emotional, irrational and helpless though sweet and lovable. Even a brief study of the role of women in various fields just in the past century or so bears out how misleading Wilde's proverb really is. One could speak of the vital part that women such as Ruth and Deborah, Joan of Arc, Queen Elizabeth, Florence Nightingale, Jane Austen and Sussana Wesley have played in the drama of world history. We are, however, going to limit ourselves almost exclusively to women's contributions during the twentieth century. The women who form the substance of this collection of biographies of great women of the past one hundred years have made their mark in the face of the prejudices reflected in the Oscar Wilde aphorism.

While the "Women's Liberation" movement and the prohibition against sexual discrimination covered under the Civil Rights Act have today begun to make things a bit easier for women, this is but a very recent phenomenon, and most of the women who are discussed in this collection were not able to benefit from this budding, progressive movement. The women of this book distinguished themselves in fields ranging from politics, religion and science to social reform, education, the arts and athletics.

They have, because of their skills and talents, enriched the twentieth century immeasurably.

These particular women have been chosen from among dozens of outstanding women in each field for several reasons. First, their biographies have a unique interest and fascination. Second, each woman has made a notable contribution to her chosen field. Third, the biography of each of these twentieth century women can be a special source of inspiration and insight. To read their stories is to derive pleasure, to gain knowledge and to develop new wisdom. The women in this collection are individuals who, because of their achievements in the face of sexual prejudice, add incalculable dimension to our own lives.

TWENTIETH CENTURY WOMEN OF ACHIEVEMENT

CHAPTER I

Mary Baker Eddy

"What man has assurance enough to
   know thoroughly the riddle of a woman's mind
and who could ever hope to fix
   her mutable nature?"

Miguel de Cervantes

Of all the institutions and movements in the history of the world, religion, more than any other, has been almost exclusively the domain of men. The greatest religious figures throughout the ages have been men such as Moses, Jesus, Martin Luther, Buddah and Mohammed. Rarely if ever have women been afforded a leadership role in religious life. In recent years, with women's increasing involvement in all phases of human endeavor, women have been ordained as rabbis and as Protestant ministers. Jewish women have conducted services as rabbis of congregations and three Presbyterian women, ordained as ministers by their church, conducted a Sunday service at the famed Riverside Church in New York and in the process scandalized the many conservative minded men and women who associated the pulpit only with the male of the species.

Yet, almost one hundred years ago, an American woman named Mary Baker Eddy founded a great religious organization —Christian Science. Part of that organization included one of America's most famous churches, one of the nationally and internationally famous newspapers, *The Christian Science Monitor,* as well as a number of other authorized publications.

Through the religious movement known as Christian Science Mary Baker Eddy challenged the existing fundamental beliefs of medicine and religion with her assertion that the "mind is all and matter is naught," that the "mind governs the body, not

Mary Baker Eddy

partially but wholly," and that "Christian Science explains all cause and effect as mental, not physical." Through radical ideas such as these she challenged mankind's perception of itself and initiated a religious movement that was to exercise a profound influence upon millions of people and on established institutions such as the church, the scientific community, the colleges and universities, and the medical profession. This doughty lady started with nothing but an idea and translated that idea into a world-wide religious organization that flourishes to this very day. The transition from an idea to a movement is synonymous with the life of Mary Baker Eddy. Among the most remarkable aspects of Mrs. Eddy's achievement was that her discovery of Christian Science did not take place until she was forty-five years old and had lived through physical and mental ill health and the ravages of two marriages.

Mary Baker was born in 1821 in Bow, New Hampshire to parents who worked a two hundred acre farm in the village to which her ancestors had come about two hundred years before in search of religious freedom. She was the youngest of the Baker family of three boys and three girls. Her father, Mark Baker, was a strong-willed man, stern and hard-working, one who broached no nonsense from his children. As a child Mary gave evidence of her future independence in several incidents.

The first instance occurred when she faced down the tall girl who was the school bully. When this intimidating youngster asked each student to drink dirty water from a hollowed cucumber, eight year old Mary Baker stood in her way and told the taller girl that she would not allow her to touch any one of her schoolmates. In the battle of wills that followed, little Mary prevailed and her antagonist backed down. This iron will, inherited from her father, with its accompanying courage and inner strength, was to dominate Mary Baker's character in later years as she singlehandedly fought to gain acceptance for her view of Christianity.

Her firm resolve also ran on a collision course with her father. While her mother was a gentle, sensitive person with whom Mary shared mutual understanding, her father was an authoritarian figure who insisted on having his way at all times. Father and daughter clashed on the subject of religion. Mary Baker was sensitive and idealistic and conceived of G-d as compassionate and loving in contrast to Mark Baker whose Calvinist religious views created a vengeful, wrathful G-d. Young as she was, Mary was unable to accept the cold, vindictive doctrines of

Calvinism. She saw life as the ultimate expression of genuine love and rational purpose.

When she was twelve Mary was questioned by her father as to the correctness of her religious views and her faith in Calvinist theology. Unable to accept a religion that was shot through with allusions to sin, damnation, and wrath, she began to argue with her father suggesting that a G-d who often condemned rather than saved and one who scolded rather than loved was not a force that she could believe in or accept. The upshot of this exchange was predictable. The battle between the strong-willed father and his iron-willed daughter raged for days as he demanded that she recant her outrageous views. But Mary was adamant, and it was only her collapse that finally brought the frightening episode to a close. Mark Baker, terrified at the prospect of possibly losing the daughter who was so much like him in many ways, rushed out to get the family doctor who urged him to leave his daughter to the care of Mrs. Baker. From then on father and daughter never clashed on matters of conscience.

Throughout her childhood Mary was sickly and nervous, given to convulsive seizures and hysterical fits. She was described as "all head and no body" because of her sensitive and idealistic nature. During those years she corresponded with her brothers who had scattered throughout the country to seek their respective fortunes. They gave her advice and the benefit of their experiences which helped her in her own development. Their encouragement sustained her for the first two decades of her life while she marked time until she could leave the farm and start a life and family of her own.

On December 12, 1843, when she was twenty-two years of age, Mary Baker married George Washington Glover, a handsome and debonair New Englander who had been trained as a mason and had started a small contracting business in Charleston, South Carolina shortly before their marriage. Mary was discomfited by the thought of living in Charleston which was a stronghold of slavery, to which she was strongly opposed, but "Wash" Glover was indifferent to the matter.

Soon after their arrival in Charleston "Wash Glover" received a contract to supply the building materials for the construction of a cathedral in Haiti, and it appeared that they might be on their way out of Charleston in short order. George Glover invested most of his money in the building materials to be shipped to Haiti and took his young wife, by now pregnant, to Wilmington, North Carolina to supervise the shipment of the building materials. Suddenly, in swift and tragic fashion, George Washington Glover was struck down with malaria. Because she was pregnant, Mary was not allowed to visit him in the hospital. A few days after he became ill George "Wash" Glover died leaving his wife almost penniless and expecting a child in three months.

Mary Baker Glover's situation was quite desperate. She was now a widowed expectant mother without any means of support. Most of her late husband's assets had been tied up in the building supplies that he had invested in for the construction of the Haitian Cathedral and those supplies had been stolen during "Wash's" week-long illness. All that was left to her were several slaves that had been given to George in payment, and since she was opposed to slavery she set them free. Destitute and ill, she returned to the home of her parents and in September, 1844 gave birth to a son whom she named George after his father.

Mary Baker Glover had always been in delicate health. The terrible ordeal which she had undergone as a result of her short-lived marriage and the subsequent birth of her son weakened her even further. She was too sick to nurse her child and little George had to be given over to a neighbor who had just lost her own child. Mrs. Glover's condition continued to deteriorate. Since she was incapable of rousing herself from her stuporlike state the raising of young George had to be assumed by a family servant. The death of Mrs. Glover's mother drove her further into the depths of despair.

In the face of all these difficulties Mrs. Glover finally began to rally. Her independent and tough spirit helped carry her through those difficult days and slowly she became convinced that suffering was evil and had to and could be overcome. Fighting her way back to some degree of emotional and physical health, she began to seek ways of supporting her infant son. Several men offered to marry her, but her sense of independence led her to decline their proposals.

Increasing pressures were exerted upon her from external sources as well. Young George was a lively and boisterous youngster and Mark Baker found that having the noisy young child around him all the time grated on his nerves. This led to new strains between father and daughter, especially after Mark Baker remarried. Mary Baker Glover had three strikes against her in seeking employment; she was a woman, she was again in poor health with a spinal condition, and she was the mother of a young child. To earn some money she taught school and sold some of her poems and essays, but her earnings from these sources were meager.

When she decided to leave her father's house Mary Baker Glover was offered a home by her wealthy sister Abigail Tilton, but only on the condition that little George not move in with them since Mrs. Tilton had a sickly child of her own and she could not cope with Mrs. Glover's energetic youngster in the same household. Mrs. Glover was forced to make an agonizing decision and she gave George up to the family servant who had since married and moved to a farm some distance away. Mrs. Glover was depressed by this turn of events, and she became obsessed with a three fold aim in life—to recover her health, to become self-supporting, and to be able to tend to her own child.

Mary Baker Glover was to spend the next two and a half years as a guest in her sister's home where she became less welcome with each passing year. Her highstrung, nervous temperament added to the burdens of her distraught family. At times she wandered about the house like a sleepwalker while at others she lay in bed rigid and immobile. Frightened by this behavior, her family catered to her every whim. As a result, she did little to help herself or to be reunited with her son. Over that difficult period Mary Baker Glover's health appeared to worsen and after a while she could no longer walk the stairs unaided, and her doctor suspected spinal paralysis. By 1850 she bore all the symptoms of a hopeless emotional and physical cripple. It seemed that only a miracle could save Mrs. Glover.

That miracle did not occur. Instead, a form of deliverance appeared in the person of Dr. Daniel Patterson, an itinerant dentist. He was an attractive, energetic man who exuded enthusiasm. Mrs. Glover and he were convinced that his vitality and love would resolve all her problems. Their marriage, however, proved to be disastrous. Since Dr. Patterson would not allow Mary Baker Patterson to have her son live with them until her physical and mental state permitted her to tend to him, Mary's condition continued to deteriorate. While Daniel Patterson loved her dearly, he was bewildered by her various moods and states and his being a poor provider and often away from home for extended periods of time compounded the various difficulties that plagued their marriage.

Even a move to Groton, New Hampshire in 1855 failed to heal their deeply wounded marriage. Mrs. Patterson's son lived nearby with his foster parents and though she occasionally tutored him, her contacts with George were rare. When George's foster parents suddenly left for Minnesota and took him with them she knew that she was losing her son forever. This episode, marked by her deep guilt feelings and frequent nervous reactions, represented one of the bleakest periods in her life. In her efforts to find a cure and inner peace Mary Baker Patterson continued her study of the Bible and also turned to homeopathy, a treatment of diseases through the minute administering of drugs which in turn produced symptoms of the disease in healthy people. Her studies led her to the conviction that faith in the drugs rather than the drugs themselves were the key to the healing process. Adding to her ever growing belief that mind and spirit were more effective than matter were popular movements in New England at that time, mesmerism (hypnosis) and spiritualism.

Mrs. Patterson's faith was tested further during the Civil War. In 1862 Dr. Daniel Patterson was assigned a dangerous mission by the governor of New Hampshire. He was asked to distribute funds to the beleaguered Southerners who were opposed to the cause of the Confederacy. Soon after he undertook this perilous mission, Daniel Patterson was captured and imprisoned. Despite his wife's valiant efforts to effect his release Dr. Patterson languished in a Confederate prison until the end of the year when he managed to escape.

During all those months of her husband's imprisonment, Mary Baker Patterson lay ill in the isolated New Hampshire village with a blind servant girl as her only companion. The women were prisoners of sorts, too—prisoners of their ill health, but the one thing that kept Mrs. Patterson going in this dark hour was her belief that deliverance was at hand. It came in the surprising form of a series of newspaper articles.

Mary Baker Patterson had read in the newspapers of the exploits of a faith healer named Phineas P. Quimby, a resident of Portland, Maine. Anxious to take advantage of his skills, she went to Portland despite her illness and poverty to meet with Quimby. By the end of her first week there she was able to walk up the eighteen steps to the dome of the Portland City Hall. It was almost miraculous, and Mary Baker Patterson was convinced that she had to learn the secret of Quimby's skills.

She began a series of intensive talks with Quimby about the source of his apparent powers. In essence his ideas reflected the popular view of the day of "mind over matter," the idea that one could control physical ailments best by destroying the patient's belief in the physical ailment. The cure lay in nature rather than drugs. One must persuade the patient that he was not sick. Through the very process of explaining his cure Quimby felt he could effect the recovery. Though he was a man with virtually no schooling, he had an almost hypnotic effect on his followers, and he was utterly convinced that he could cure and heal in the same way that Jesus had. Mrs. Patterson was caught up in Quimby's inspiring presentation and by his magnetic personality. They began to exchange notes and ideas. She was convinced of the role of divine power in all manifestations of faith healing, but she still did not understand the nature and effects of that divine power. Still unanswered was the fundamental question of how someone could call up these powers at will. She wondered what basic rule of healing could be derived from her recent experiences? Mary Baker Patterson became obsessed with the subject of spiritual healing, and she soon became a powerful orator and writer on behalf of this health cure. For the first time in many years she was a self-confident, fulfilled, and vigorous woman. It was at this time that Dr. Patterson returned to Portland after his escape from a Confederate prison. Now he was ill and in need of someone to take care of him.

They decided to move to Lynn, Massachusetts where Mary, now healthy and energetic, tried to make a new life for them. It was an ill-fated attempt. Daniel Patterson could not cope with a wife now burning with evangelical zeal and soon his restlessness returned and the two began to quarrel bitterly. In 1863 Mary Baker Patterson was deserted by Dr. Patterson and found herself living alone and facing a financial and personal crisis.

For several years she imposed herself upon the tender mercies of various individuals with whom she lived for the sake of simple survival. These years of deprivation and solitude forced her to probe more deeply into her own ideas and emotions, and she began to develop a coherent philosophy of her own on the subject of healing. A dramatic event in February, 1866 in Lynn, Massachusetts provided the catalyst which was to propel her into becoming the head of a nationwide religious movement.

While returning from a meeting on a blustery February night she slipped on the ice and fell to the ground with such violence that she lost consciousness. Friends who were with her carried her to a nearby house and called a doctor. The doctor diagnosed her injuries as a serious head concussion and a severe spinal injury. She would never walk again. In all likelihood Mrs. Patterson would remain an invalid for the rest of her life. For two days she lay in a coma, but on the third day she woke, asked for a Bible and requested that she be left alone. As she glanced at the Bible her eye fell upon the passage in Matthew, Chapter IX, verses 2–9, which related the account of Jesus' curing the paralyzed man: ". . . and Jesus said to the paralytic, Be of good cheer, child; thy sins are forgiven . . . Arise, . . . go unto thy house. And he arose, and went away to his house." It was through these words and others such as, "Behold I set before you this day death or life, blessing or curse. Choose," that Mary discovered "the Science of divine metaphysical healing." According to Mary Baker Patterson's own versions of the incident, her reading of these passages from the Bible and their revelation of the mysteries of divine healing had such a profound impact upon her that she got up out of bed and walked into the next room where her friends waited anxiously. When they saw her they were overwhelmed. They had expected that their friend would be either hopelessly crippled or dead. This smiling, healthy individual was more of an apparition than a real human being to them.

Mary Baker Patterson had discovered Christian Science. Life now had new meaning and purpose for her. A twenty year search was coming to an end. Now she had to devote her time to absorbing and understanding the implications of the several experiences that had dramatically changed her physical condition as well as her perceptions of life.

For the next three years she led a particularly lonely and desperate life as she struggled to evolve a coherent philosophy and a workable program centered around the experiences that she had just undergone. She now conceived of G-d and the Mind as being one and the same, and personal health as a phenomenon that emerged from faith and universal love. Convinced that Jesus' injunction "Go ye unto the world and heal the sick," was of significance for every Christian, she searched for the lost secret of healing, the program that she could give to all humanity.

Her three year mission was complicated to a considerable degree by continuing personal misfortune. She was separated from Daniel Patterson and would soon have to undergo the agony of divorce proceedings, and she led a precarious existence as she moved from one boardinghouse to another with her only friends being the factory hands in Lynn. It was these people upon whom she often tried out her ideas and practices. Her activities and almost unbroken string of successes led to considerable notoriety and she was the target of several attacks and investigations.

In October, 1867 Mrs. Patterson reached the nadir of her misfortunes after she found herself homeless, alone, and penniless in Amesbury, Massachusetts. On a cold, uncomfortable night she was taken in by Mrs. Nathaniel Webster, the wife of a retired sea captain. Mary Baker Patterson was able to stay with the kind old lady for several months while she worked on a commentary of the Bible that would reveal the meaning of her experiences. That summer Mrs. Patterson was turned out of Mrs. Webster's house by the old lady's son-in-law. While a rainstorm raged outside, Mary Baker Patterson sat stunned and shivering, contemplating her next move. Just then she was joined on the front stoop by Richard Kennedy, a young boarder in Mrs. Webster's house who had been impressed by her ideas. Out of compassion for her and because of his interest in her ideas he offered her a place to stay with a Miss Bagley to whom he was related.

Both Mary Baker Patterson and Richard Kennedy were taken in by Miss Bagley. She too was interested in mind science and so both Miss Bagley and Richard Kennedy became her most avid students. Richard Kennedy, an apt student, became so proficient in Mrs. Patterson's teaching that he left his factory job and became a full time faith healer. In 1870 Mrs. Patterson and Richard Kennedy rented space over a kindergarten to expand their activities. Their plans called for Richard to do the healing

while Mrs. Patterson did the teaching. Their efforts were successful almost from the start for they soon had twelve students enrolled in the course of twelve lessons for a total of $300.

As a teacher Mary Baker Patterson was provocative but simultaneously firm and usually convincing in her views. Speaking
with complete confidence and authority, she stated to her pupils
that true mental healing had to be purely spiritual, divorced
from any material aids such as drugs or the "laying on of hands."
Richard Kennedy, her partner in the school, believed in the latter
practice particularly and so, because of this philosophical differ-
ence as well as personality clashes, they decided upon the dissolution of the partnership and he went off to start a practice of his
own elsewhere in Lynn. What Mary Baker Patterson had called
"Moral Science" was now a doctrine on its way to being given
its final name of "Christian Science." This marked the beginning
of a new solitary period in Mary Baker Patterson's life, devoted
totally to preaching and practicing her doctrine. Christian
Science from this point on was posited as mental healing powered
exclusively by faith. Christian Science fused religion and reason,
faith and science.

In 1875 one of Mary Baker Patterson's major projects came
to fruition. Since 1867 she had been writing a book that was to
be the cornerstone of her doctrine. Throughout the eight year
period during which the book was written she had wandered
from boardinghouse to boardinghouse, had suffered from abject
poverty and frequent bouts of illness. The book, *Science and
Health with Key to the Scriptures,* emerged as an act of faith as
well as a religious and institutional credo because no publisher
would venture to publish a book on so controversial and risky a
subject as faith healing. With her fanatical drive and personal
charisma she was able to inspire two of her students to put up the
$2,200 that was necessary to produce a run of one thousand cop-
ies under the imprint of the Christian Science Publishing Company in Boston.

The book was afforded respectable treatment by a number of
newspaper book reviewers but it went largely unnoticed. Her

students, though, carried the burden of bringing the book to the attention of the general public. The book was sold door to door, a newspaper advertising campaign was effected, and copies were sent to prominent individuals, universities and libraries. The marketing campaign began to take effect and soon the book was being widely circulated, its circulation and readership among people of various backgrounds being greater than its actual sales. Among her admirers was Bronson Alcott, the famous philosopher and teacher, friend of Ralph Waldo Emerson and father of Louisa May Alcott who wrote *Little Women*. Other advocates were Edward Everett Hale, the most influential preacher in Boston and Wendell Phillips, an assistant to famous abolitionist William Lloyd Garrison. Her book and the healing successes of her followers were slowly but surely building a vast army of "true believers."

Science and Health to the non-believer is almost simplistic in its approach. Many lines would challenge the credibility of most authors and the faith of many readers. Mary Baker Patterson wrote that "the Divine Principle of healing is proved in the personal experience of any sincere seeker for Truth . . . Christian Science rationally explains that all other pathological methods are the fruits of human faith in matter—faith in the workings, not of Spirit, but of fleshly mind which must yield to Science. . . . Mind is all and matter is naught as the leading factor in Mind-science. . . . Mind governs the body, not partially but wholly. . . . Christian Science explains all cause and effect as mental, not physical." She rejected the idea of illness and evil since G-d is synonymous with spiritual strength and goodness. Despite the simplistic and, to many people, incredible quality of the basic tenets of Christian Science, it gained wide acceptance. This can probably be attributed to its very simplicity and comprehensibility, its relatively undemanding character as well as its having drawn heavily from many basic tenets of Christianity.

Christian Science was soon in the process of being expanded and institutionalized. In 1876 the Christian Science Association was formed. Its purpose was to arrange for weekly meetings in various Massachusetts cities including Boston, Lynn, Roxbury and Salem. At that time one of Mary Baker Patterson's most promising students was Asa Gilbert Eddy who had enrolled in her school because she had him healed of a bad infection. Having finished her course, he became the first "Christian science practitioner" and also a great help to his teacher who was heavily burdened by her responsibilities as a teacher, healer and administrator. His practical nature along with his grasp of administrative detail made him almost indispensable to her. Soon the exhausted, lonely, overdriven and strong-willed fifty-six year old woman found that she needed both Gilbert Eddy's moral and emotional support as well as his organizational skills. On January 1, 1877 they were married.

Their marriage was a happy and satisfying one, but the controversy and pressure that emanated from their work with Christian Science gave them little respite. Some of Mary Baker Eddy's students wanted to present Christian Science in an aggressive, sensational manner in contrast with her desire for it to emerge in rational, deliberate fashion. Law suits began to crop up, and Gilbert Eddy, in one particularly ugly situation, was accused of a conspiracy to murder. He was acquitted of the charges but the atmosphere that resulted from these many confrontations made Lynn too unpleasant a setting in which to function comfortably. In 1879 Mary Baker Eddy organized the First Church of Christ, Scientist in Boston, and in 1882 she and her husband left Lynn for Boston.

In Boston Mary and Gilbert Eddy expanded their Christian Science activities. The First Church of Christ, Scientist was put on a firm footing and in 1882 they opened in Massachusetts Metaphysical College which was created to handle the ever increasing numbers of people who were interested in training as practitioners of Christian Science. The course textbook was Mary Baker Eddy's own book, *Science and Health*. The college was a great success from its inception. By now sixty-two years of age, Mary Baker Eddy was still a highly effective teacher preaching her doctrine of Christian Science as a scientific system of divine healing and belief in the supremacy of mind and spirit over matter and body. Mary Baker Eddy's life now appeared to take on a quality of tranquility and fulfillment uncharacteristic of much of those preceding years. Then with swift and terrible suddenness that happy time came to an end. Asa Gilbert Eddy became ill and died on June 3, 1882. Emotionally shattered and guilt ridden by his death since she felt she should have taken the time out to heal him herself, she ran off to Vermont in search of seclusion. After several days however, she returned composed and ready to meet her many obligations.

Over the course of the next decade Mary Baker Eddy engaged in a schedule of activities which would have exhausted the efforts of a whole complement of women. In April, 1883 she founded *The Christian Science Journal* which was to become one of the most important periodicals published by the movement. She had to fend off the attacks of the orthodox, established churches which branded her a charlatan and a heretic. She preached almost every Sunday and lectured every Thursday. In 1898 she founded the Christian Science Publishing Society.

Mary Baker Eddy was sensitive to the possibility that the doctrine of Christian Science could deteriorate into a movement that was more of a personality cult than a viable religious doctrine. A huge and rather raucous crowd that gathered in June, 1888 in Chicago to hear her deliver a brilliant exposition on the basic tenets of Christian Science convinced her that the movement was growing too quickly and too erratically. For some nine years she went into retreat in Concord, New Hampshire where she led a relatively quiet, contemplative existence.

Those years from 1889 to 1908 were still not without their demands upon her time and energy. She aided her students in their efforts to build the Mother Church in Boston, one that would draw its membership from Christian Scientists from all over the world. Ever vigilant against the cult of personality and the possibility of poor organization, she collated all of the practices and rules of the movement into the *Church Manual,* a practical guide to the sound governance of the Christian Science movement. On two separate occasions during those years the Massachusetts State legislature tried to put through a bill that would restrain Christian Science but both attempts failed. Christian Science had developed legions of admirers and adherents, and by 1900 Christian Science churches were developing at a rapid rate. Even Mark Twain, who had originally been hostile to Christian Science, had become a supporter.

The rapidity of the growth of Christian Science was seen most notably in Boston in 1902. The Boston Church was now much too small for the demands of the movement and, as a mark of tribute to their adored leader, Christian Scientists throughout the land launched a two million dollar building fund campaign which was rapidly oversubscribed. Four years later, in 1906, some forty thousand visitors from all over the country attended six separate dedication services organized to accommodate them. Mary Baker Eddy, by then eighty-five years old, was at the center of everyone's thoughts though she was unable to attend the ceremonies because of her advanced age and poor health.

Though she was an old woman she was still a lightning rod for attacks and controversy. Joseph Pulitzer, at that time probably the best known and most powerful newspaper publisher in the country, launched a savage personal attack against her. The Pulitzer newspaper chain charged her with incompetence and senility and suggested that she was incapable of handling her own affairs. They asserted that she was being exploited by an unscrupulous group of individuals who were out to take advantage of her fame and wealth.

The peace and quiet of Concord was suddenly shattered by an invasion of Pulitzer reporters anxious to find sensational details about Mary Baker Eddy's associates and organization. They came to Concord expecting to see a doddering old lady. Instead they were met by a poised, articulate and attractive older woman who handled the crisis with her customary aplomb. The charges and accusations collapsed like a house of cards and soon the judges, lawyers and reporters left Concord convinced of her mental competence.

Concord had lost its idyllic quality and so in January, 1908 she returned to Boston. Though eighty-seven, she made yet another contribution to the vitality of Christian Science. She began work on another important project, creating a new daily newspaper. *The Christian Science Monitor* was established in January, 1908 and it gradually assumed the position in which it remains today among the greatest newspapers in the country if not the world. Almost to the end of her days Mary Baker Eddy continued to make important contributions to the movement and to the nation.

The last two years of her life were spent in relative calm and privacy in Boston. She lived quietly and limited her trips outside the house to an occasional drive around her suburban Boston home. At the age of ninety she waited for death with serenity, for she felt that death was not the end, but the beginning of life. On December 3, 1910 she died quietly in Boston.

Mary Baker Eddy's life was filled with tragedy, frustration, unhappiness, and controversy; yet, she managed to overcome all the haters and the doubters. Her ideas and her movement, though considered incredible by many people, continue to flourish to this very day. Her life is an impressive example of the power of an idea, and its effects upon one brilliant and charismatic individual who was able to transmit a doctrine into a meaningful way of life for myriads of people.

A CURRENT BIBLIOGRAPHY

The bibliography listed below contains books in two broad areas. The first part contains a list of books about Mary Baker Eddy. The second contains a list of books attributed to her authorship.

Books About Mary Baker Eddy

Wilbur, Sibyl. *The Life of Mary Baker Eddy*. Boston: The Christian Science Publishing Society, 1907.

Daken, E. F. *Mrs. Eddy: The Biography of a Virginal Mind*. New York: Charles Scribner and Son, 1929.

Johnston, J. M. *Mary Baker Eddy: Her Mission and Triumph*. Boston: The Christian Science Publishing Society, 1946.

King, Marion. *Mary Baker Eddy: Child of Promise*. Englewood: Prentice-Hall, 1968.

Peel, Robert. *Mary Baker Eddy*. New York: Holt Rinehart and Winston, Vol. I 1966, Vol. II 1971.

Zweig, Stefan. *Mental Healers–Mesmer, Mary Baker Eddy, Freud*. New York: Frederick Ungar Publishing Co., 1932.

Books by Mary Baker Eddy

Science and Health with Key to the Scriptures. Boston: Published by the Trustees Under the Will of Mary Baker Eddy, 1875.

Miscellaneous Writings

The First Church of Christ Scientist and Miscellany
Church Manual
Unity of Good
Christian Healing
No and Yes
Retrospection and Introspection
Christian Science Versus Panthesism
Rudimental Divine Science
People's Idea of G-d
Christ and Christmas
Pulpit and Press
Message to The Mother Church, 1900
Message to The Mother Church, 1901
Message to The Mother Church, 1902
Poems

CHAPTER II

Mary McLeod Bethune

"how divine a thing
A woman may be made."
William Wordsworth

On July 10, 1974 more than 20,000 people from all over the United States witnessed the unveiling of the Mary McLeod Bethune Memorial in Washington, D.C. This was the first monument to a black person or a woman on public land in the nation's capital. The newspaper accounts of the ceremonies did not indicate in detail why this woman, Mary McLeod Bethune, should be so honored nearly two decades after her death. As one learns about her life the honor and the occasion take on greater meaning.

The doors of college education opportunities were virtually closed to young blacks in this country for many decades. One of the prime movers in developing opportunities in higher education for blacks was a gifted and tenacious black woman named Mary McLeod Bethune. During the course of her lifetime she succeeded in a variety of important assignments, a tribute to her versatility and her devotion. Her most significant achievement though, was her life's work in establishing a small school that developed under her energetic leadership into Bethune-Cookman College, an outstanding institution of higher learning for young blacks. She began her life as one of a family of seventeen children born to two former slaves, but later became a member of the administration of President Franklin Delano Roosevelt. Her story is a classic example of the actualization of the American Dream.

Mary Jane McLeod's parents and her older brothers and sisters were slaves on plantations in South Carolina. She was born on July 10, 1875, fifteenth child of a family of seventeen, but the first of the children to be born in freedom. After the Civil War Samuel McLeod, Mary Jane's father, managed to earn enough money to buy thirty-five acres of land with a wood cabin on it. The only other material possessions the family possessed were a cow, a mule and a plow. Mary Jane McLeod's early memories were mainly of back-breaking labor as all members of the family—parents, grandparents and children—cut cotton and rice and chopped up fodder for the animals. The children worked at a variety of chores to help the family keep body and soul together. By the time she was nine years of age Mary Jane McLeod could pick two hundred and fifty pounds of cotton a day.

One year the McLeod children had to assume a chore that was particularly memorable and numbing. When the overworked old mule literally dropped dead in the middle of a furrow that he had just plowed, the older children had to take turns trying to pull the plow! They had to become to all intents and purposes beasts of burden so that the family could have enough food to eat.

The four room shack that was home for this large brood was sustained by prayer and the simple faith that was expressed daily by the children's grandmother, Sophia. Mary Jane McLeod's grandmother spoke to G-d all day as if He were actually present. Both she and the young girl's mother often expressed their gratitude to G-d. It was the presence of G-d that helped to sustain the family during its years of almost unbelievable toil.

To the physical pain of that toil was added the psychological trauma of the Southern lynch mob which operated against blacks. Young Mary McLeod once watched horror stricken as an unruly, hate filled mob of whites began the process of "stringing up" a black man who had reacted to the goading of a white man and had struck him. As the horrible preliminaries took place, Mary Jane McLeod was pulled away by her father so that she would be spared the awful sight. Though she did not see the actual lynching, Mary Jane was in a state of shock for a long time afterwards.

Education was out of the question and out of mind for the McLeod children. They were all needed on the farm to help produce the crops and the produce that stood between them and starvation. Yet Mary Jane McLeod who had been termed "different" by her family was to show how really different she was by being the first of the McLeods to receive a formal education.

One day Mary Jane accompanied her mother to the house of a former mistress to whom she was delivering laundry. In the house the young black girl saw, among the grandchildren's toys, an object that was unfamiliar to her. When she picked it up, she was told by one of the white children to put the book down, since she couldn't read. Stung by embarassment, Mary Jane McLeod resolved to learn to read someday. Her chance came soon after that incident. It was to be the beginning of a lifelong love affair between Mary Jane McLeod and learning.

A Miss Wilson, who had been assigned the Mission Board of the Presbyterian Church to start a school for black children, appeared in Mayesville, North Carolina shortly after the book incident had occurred. She went from cabin to cabin to convince parents to allow their children to attend school. Mr. McLeod was one of the parents who agreed. It was a decision that was to have far-reaching consequences upon the lives of hundreds of thousands of young black people. Out of that decision was born a woman who became one of the most effective and influential workers for improving the social, economic and educational positions of young blacks in the history of our nation.

Excited at the prospect of being taught to read, the young girl was up at dawn the following day. Wearing new brogans with copper toes, a sun bonnet and shawl, and carrying a slate and piece of chalk and a lunch pail containing bread and milk, she trudged the five miles to school on foot. Every day for the next six years Mary Jane McLeod made the ten mile round trip, uncomplaining and enthusiastic, spurred by her desire to read and anxious to overcome the embarrassment her illiteracy had previously caused her. Mary Jane stayed at the Mayesville Institute through the elementary grades. By the time she was fifteen she had absorbed all the learning that she had been exposed to and faced the prospect of returning to the farm and a life of backbreaking labor. The bright teen-aged girl yearned to continue her education and become a teacher like Miss Wilson. She had already shown a feel for the teaching profession by her efforts to teach her brothers and sisters to read and to write. The family's desperate financial situation seemed to preclude the possibility of her furthering her education. For about a year Mary Jane McLeod went back to the grind of picking cotton and working in the fields.

The promising young woman's faith in her future was unwavering though, and one day her prayers appeared to be answered. Miss Wilson came to her with the good news that a white woman in Denver, Colorado had heard about the fine work being done in the Mayesville Mission School, and she was prepared to provide a scholarship to further the education of a worthy graduate. The school had chosen Mary Jane McLeod and she was to attend the Scotia Seminary, a school for black girls in Concord, North Carolina where Miss Wilson had received her own training. The entire community turned out to see Mary Jane McLeod off when she left by train. Fate had singled her out for an important mission.

The Scotia Seminary in Concord, North Carolina was a revelation for Mary Jane. She had never seen a brick building before nor had she ever been exposed to the refinements that were in evidence there such as steps, white table cloths, fine cutlery and glassware. She was to remain at the Scotia Seminary for seven years and learned a variety of subjects such as algebra, Greek and Latin that were completely new to her, as well as a whole new life style.

This new life style notwithstanding, Mary Jane McLeod had to work her way through school. The scholarship barely covered her tuition and board at the Scotia Seminary. Since she could not afford to go home during the holidays or during the summers, she worked to earn money for her personal needs. She worked as a cook, laundress, nurse, farm girl or chambermaid to keep going. At one point she had only one dress to wear and she resorted to washing it out overnight to wear again the next day until she found some castoff clothing in one of the barrels of clothing that had been sent as charity to the school.

At the end of her seven years of study Mary Jane McLeod had decided upon a career as a missionary to Africa. There were, however, no openings for Negro missionaries in Africa, and it was a bitter disappointment for the idealistic young woman. Instead she applied for and went on to Chicago to study at the Moody Bible Institute where she studied Bible and did field work in tending to the sick and to the poor, conducting religious services in the local prisons and even doing evangelical work in dangerous slum areas of Chicago. After two years at the Moody Bible Institute Mary Jane McLeod tried once again to get a missionary assignment to Africa but she was rebuffed. She then turned to teaching.

For one year she returned to Mayesville where she worked as an assistant to Miss Wilson and from there she went on to the Haines Normal Institute in Augusta, Georgia as an eighth grade teacher. During her one year there she learned a great deal about enlivening and recruiting students for school in a slum area. Her inspiration at the Haines Institute was a pioneer Negro educator named Lucey Laney who taught her that working for the education of black children in America was as important as being a missionary to the Negroes in Africa. There the young teacher learned how to cope with her students' problems of poverty, family instability, malnutrition and disease. At the end of a year she transferred to another school for Negro children in Sumter, Georgia. That seven year period after she left the Moody Bible Institute in Chicago also included teaching stints in Savannah, Georgia and Palatka, Florida. Mary Jane McLeod received very sound fundamental teaching and administrative experience during those professionally formative years.

During her service in Savannah, Georgia Mary Jane McLeod's life took another turn. She met, fell in love with and married Alburtus Bethune, a teaching colleague. A son was born to the young couple while Albertus Bethune taught in Savannah and Mary McLeod Bethune, as she was now called and known, dropped out of teaching for a year. The Bethune family then moved to Florida where Mary McLeod Bethune developed a passion for starting her own school, one which she could organize, and control. It would be the channel through which she could funnel the energies and ideals that she wished to devote to bettering the education of black children in America. The second act of the dramatic life story of Mary McLeod Bethune was about to begin.

Mary McLeod Bethune's family life also took a dramatic turn at this point. She and Albertus had differed over the move to Daytona Beach. He felt strongly that the plan was impractical since their financial resources tallied up to the meager sum of $1.50. Despite Albertus' objections and their almost penniless state, Mary was determined to go and so she packed a few things for herself and for young Albert and went to Daytona Beach. She told Albertus that when she was settled there she would write him to come to Daytona Beach if he so desired. It was only several years later that Albertus came to visit with his family for a few months. He went fishing with his son, discussed Albert's education and future with Mary, and sang in the chapel chorus, but he found himself at loose ends. The school was Mary's creation and her life. When the fall term began Albertus left Daytona Beach. Until his death five years later he taught in a boys' school in Georgia, and he and Mary maintained a friendly relationship, but he never returned to the school. For a man of his particular temperament and a woman with her strong will and single-mindedness, it was to be an ill-fated marriage.

She sought to establish a school for black children, but in a new area, and she set out to determine which community would provide the most productive setting for a new school. She learned that the Florida East Coast railroad would be extended down the state and with it would come thousands of black workers and their families. Daytona Beach, Florida seemed to be the most suitable location for Mrs. Bethune to realize her dream for it was a growing resort town as well as the home of a substantial black population, most of whom were living in unbelievable squalor. It was here then that she decided to begin the process of cultivating her dream.

Hers was an effort that was grounded more in faith and energy than it was in money or material goods. When she finally found the site for her school Mrs. Bethune was virtually penniless, yet the owner allowed her to rent the run down four room house on credit, hoping that Mrs. Bethune would be able to meet the monthly rental of eleven dollars. The cottage was an empty shell, devoid of any equipment, furnishings, or supplies. Undaunted, Mary McLeod Bethune went about the business of setting up her schoolhouse.

With boxes and packing cases that she had begged from neighboring stores to serve as pupils' chairs and desks, and an upended barrel as her own chair, and with an opening pupil register of five young girls and her son, Mary McLeod Bethune opened her school. The Daytona Educational and Industrial Training School for Negro Girls went into action on October 4, 1904. It was to be the precursor of what was eventually to become Bethune-Cookman College. Parents paid fifty cents tuition per week if they had the money. Mrs. Bethune not only administered and taught in the school, but she also had to raise money and materials to keep it in operation. She salvaged anything usable from the city dump and the resort hotels, items such as cracked dishes, used lumber, old linens and old lamps. Logs were burned and the charred splinters served as pencils; elderberries were mashed and used for ink. The ever resourceful principal-teacher used these experiences as learning opportunities for her young charges. If they were to be trained in the areas of

crafts, homemaking and other salable skills, what better laboratory or shop could they find?

Food, crockery and furniture was often brought to the school
as a form of barter and gratitude. On one occasion, just before
Christmas, when they were sorely in need of a set of dishes, a
set arrived at the school given by a woman whose son had just
presented her with a new set. Once two men in prison uniforms
came up to the school bearing a gift of produce, groceries and
cash in gratitude for the Sunday singing services that had been
conducted at the prison by the school's student body.

Mrs. Bethune's skills as a fund raiser were also quite formidable. She made pies and sold them to the railroad track laborers
and even received four dollars from a group of Negro laborers
who had received the benefits of adult education courses in the
school some weeks before. The money came at a propitious time
because she needed that sum of money to meet a grocery bill.

The school grew rapidly, and in two years its student body
had grown from five to two hundred and fifty; substantial funds
and new buildings were required. With the kind of faith and self
confidence that were her hallmark, Mary McLeod Bethune
worked hard at meeting that twofold need. She organized fund
raising campaigns using her students as workers, she prepared
literature, she spoke at churches, lodges and mansions to espouse
her cause. Soon another building was rented next door, but Mrs.
Bethune recognized that the school needed to buy a piece of
land on which it could erect a building of its own. That dream
was soon to be realized and in a rather unlikely place.

She found a piece of land at the edge of the Negro section of
town right next to the city dump. Since "beggars can't be choos-
ers," Mrs. Bethune decided to purchase the land for two hundred
dollars, five dollars as a down payment with the rest to be paid
over the next two years. A large number of pies and ice cream
was sold over the next few years to help meet those payments.
The school was now well along the route to expansion.

To fund and organize her expanding school Mrs. Bethune
drew upon the financial resources and business acumen of the

many wealthy tourists who frequented Daytona Beach. She wrote to and visited with many of them who were guests at the Daytona Beach tourist hotels or who lived in luxurious estates nearby. Soon she was able to prevail upon a member of wealthy and influential businessmen, among them James N. Gamble of Proctor and Gamble soap and Thomas H. White, the automobile and machine manufacturer, to become trustees and financial supporters of the school. They were astonished when they first saw the four room shack schoolhouse and the city dump expansion site, but they were also deeply moved by the pluck and the dedication of Mrs. Bethune. Their contributions soon began in amounts ranging from a pittance of 25¢ to sums as high as $67,000. They also were influential in persuading many of their friends to contribute to the school's support and to become members of its board of trustees.

The swampy piece of land was paid for and cleared and by 1907 its first building, appropriately named "Faith Hall," was erected. Above the entrance to the four story structure were inscribed the words "Enter to Learn" and over the inside door was written the legend "Depart to Serve." The building had been built in part with secondhand bricks and other construction materials that the doughty principal had begged from local contractors. The work had been done by black construction workers who volunteered their services on their off hours and weekends as part or whole payment for their children's tuition. Even in the process of expansion the school continued to be the product of cooperative efforts linked together to meet ever present crises. Now, however, the school with a new building and a student body of some four hundred pupils, was really launched on its flight to becoming Bethune-Cookman College.

The painful daily struggles for survival continued despite the support of its many benefactors. Financial worries, pressing bills, adamant creditors, ever present demands kept pressing in on the school and Mrs. Bethune but she remained unflappable in the face of a host of problems. Even when they had to contend with the hostility of whites who resented the idea of blacks getting an education and possibly losing their sense of place in the southern caste system, Mrs. Bethune continued serenely to educate students. When a group of hooded and white-robed Ku Klux Klansmen carrying torches marched in front of the school the night before Election Day, Mrs. Bethune insisted that every light in the buildings be turned on as a mark of confidence and defiance. The next day the black people of Daytona Beach, led by Mrs. Bethune, went to the polls and voted despite their being forced to wait all day. They were not to be intimidated.

There were differing philosophies among black educators about the nature and goals of education for black youth. There were those who asserted that young blacks should be given a liberal arts college education while others argued that they should be given sound career and vocational training. Booker T. Washington, the famed black educator-scientist, subscribed to the latter view and was attacked by many of his colleagues. Mrs. Bethune also took Booker T. Washington's view because she felt that in everyday life blacks would need training in skills such as food and health care, farming, and crafts of various sorts. She felt the academic skills beyond the fundamentals were frills that were unnecessary and impractical for blacks who had to face the harsh realities of the job market of the day.

Amidst these various crises and controversies Mrs. Bethune's dream continued to bloom and to flourish. The borders surrounding the city dump were turned into flower and vegetable gardens. Many new buildings were erected and over the decades the school grew at a steady pace. By 1911 a high school curriculum was added, and in 1925 the Cookman Institute of Jacksonville, Florida, a boys' school, merged with Mrs. Bethune's creation as the Daytona Cookman Collegiate Institute. Shortly thereafter, in honor of the woman who was the school's inspiration and driving force, the school's name was changed to its present one. Bethune-Cookman College now has some twenty-seven buildings and a plant valued at well over one million dollars, a faculty of over one hundred teachers and scholars, a student body that exceeds one thousand, most of whom go on to become teachers themselves. Today it is one of the most important and highly regarded colleges of the deep South, having received an "A" rating from a major accrediting agency, the Southern Association of Colleges and Secondary Schools.

But Mary McLeod Bethune's energies and talents were not confined solely to the school she had created. Shortly after taking office in 1934, President Roosevelt invited Mrs. Bethune to come to Washington, D.C. to serve in his administration as a Director of the Division of Negro Affairs in the National Youth Administration. It was at that time the highest position ever held in government by a black woman, and for eight years the forceful and effective administrator of this program was able to provide for the education or employment of tens of thousands of black youths who otherwise might have been condemned to a life of ignorance and poverty. In one year alone she was able to arrange for emergency classes for 600,000 rural black children where they were taught academic fundamentals and vocational skills.

In 1935, while serving with the Roosevelt Administration, Mrs. Bethune organized the National Council of Negro Women, an organization that united almost all of the black women's clubs of America. The organization, which numbered approximately eight hundred thousand women, took as its main objectives the betterment of blacks' status in America and better relations between blacks and whites. The council's work occupied a major part of Mrs. Bethune's energies during the latter years of her life. By virtue of her position she had become in effect the leader of all black women in America.

During those last two decades of her life Mary McLeod Bethune was a vigorous and forceful proponent of equal rights and dignity for blacks. She was by no means a shrinking violet; she once told President Roosevelt that he had to do more for blacks, and on another occasion, publicly berated the white chairman of a meeting of the Southern Conference on Human Welfare for referring to her by her first name, a subconscious racist slur, as all white delegates were called by their surnames.

She amassed during those years an array of positions, assignments, titles, honorary degrees, and organization memberships that are almost mind boggling. Aside from her work in creating Bethune-Cookman College she wrote weekly newspaper columns, chapters in books, articles in periodicals, served in Federal and wartime positions under Presidents Coolidge, Hoover, Roosevelt, and Truman, and was an officer and member of organizations ranging from the American Teachers' Association, National Association of Colored Women, N.A.A.C.P., Urban League, the General Conference of the Methodist Church, the Planned Parent Federation of America, the Girl Scouts of America and the Delinquent Home for Colored Girls in Ocala, Florida. Mrs. Bethune was awarded honorary degrees by many universities and colleges, among them Rollins College, Wilberforce University, Howard University and the Tuskeegee Institute. Though occupied as a president, founder or member of various professional, civic, religious, political action and social service organizations, this extraordinary lady also found time to serve in executive business positions with life insurance companies and other ventures and to be a member of a number of clubs and sororities such as the Daughters of the Elks, Delta Sigma Theta and Lamba Kappa Mu. She even found time to travel extensively throughout the United States and Europe and to pursue her hobbies of collecting photographs of famous men and women, model elephants and walking canes of famous men. Mary McLeod Bethune was the very personification of productivity and versatility.

During her last years Mrs. Bethune returned to the Bethune-Cookman College campus to enjoy some rest and serenity with her son, her grandchildren and her great grandchildren. Surrounded by the monuments to her creative genius, she basked in the knowledge that her labors had borne rich fruit. By the time of her death in the mid-fifties more than a hundred Negro colleges and universities in the United States enrolled over seventy-five thousand students on various levels of study. Tens of thousands of blacks have been graduated from institutions of higher learning with degrees ranging from the B.A. to the Ph.D. and M.D. degree. Tens of thousands of them are skilled workmen, businessmen, professionals and artists. In contrast, when Mary Jane McLeod Bethune was a child, fewer than five per cent of the black population were literate. In her lifetime the black literacy rate rose to over ninety per cent, and the idea of black children going to school became an accepted fact of life. She played a seminal role in her people's progress towards achieving a dignified, full life, though they are still a long way from achieving social, economic, and political equality with the white population of this country.

On the afternoon of May 18, 1955 Mrs. Bethune sat on the front porch of her home on the college campus gently rocking in her chair. She got up, went into the house, and suddenly collapsed and died. Her death was quick and quiet in marked contrast to her long, often painful and crisis ridden struggle to make her people's and her own life replete with dignity and opportunity. She was in her eightieth year when she died, but her works live on. As long as Bethune-Cookman College and its graduates live, as long as the organizations to which she devoted her energies continue to function, Mary McLeod Bethune will continue to remain a vital force on the American national scene.

A CURRENT BIBLIOGRAPHY

Carruth, E. K. *She Wanted to Read*. New York: Abingdon Press, 1966 (Juvenile).

Holt, Rackham. *Mary McLeod Bethune—A Biography*. New York: Doubleday and Company, Inc., 1964.

Peare, Catherine Owens. *Mary McLeod Bethune*. New York: Vanguard Press, 1951.

Radford, Ruby I. *Mary M. Bethune*. New York: Putnam, 1973 (Juvenile).

Sterne, E. M. *Mary McLeod Bethune*. New York: Knopf, 1957.

CHAPTER III

Margaret Sanger

"Woman's at best a contradiction still"
Alexander Pope

International concern about the population explosion, and the raging controversy that surrounds women's rights to practice birth control and to have an abortion, are high on the list of the most emotionally debated subjects in our country. The dangers inherent in overpopulation and the shrinking food supply in drought ridden lands of West Africa and the sub-Sahara and various Asian nations, as well as the civil and religious rights issue of women's prerogatives regarding their bodies have been widely discussed, particularly during the past several years. One of the most famous adherents of birth control in the world was Margaret Sanger, and her views immersed her in controversy during the early decades of this century. Her courageous and pioneering stand on an emotionally, socially, economically, religiously and politically charged issue resulted in her arrest, conviction and imprisonment. Her struggle to disseminate birth control information to women, which she began over sixty years ago, was a precursor to the present day struggles of women to achieve political and social parity, to prevent world-wide poverty and starvation and to create international awareness of the perils of an unrestricted birth rate. As the pioneer of the birth control movement, this indomitable woman helped to unleash forces that are having a profound effect on the life and thinking of people throughout the world.

PHOTO COURTESY PLANNED PARENTHOOD-WORLD POPULATION

Margaret Sanger

Margaret Higgins, one of eleven children, was born in 1879 in Corning, New York. She was the sixth child born in the family, and while still a child herself, she helped in the delivery of every brother and sister born after her. By the time she was a teenager birth and sex were no mystery to her. Her parents were both

Irish immigrants. Michael Higgins, Margaret's father, was a stone cutter who earned a precarious living carving out figures of angels and saints on gravestones in the local Catholic cemetery. He was a veteran of the Civil War, a frustrated sculptor and an outspoken radical and free thinker. Erratic and generous to a fault, he would bring home eight children as guests for dinner into a crowded and poverty stricken household, buy dinner for fifty at a banquet at which Henry George, proponent of the single tax, spoke, and give out bananas to every child in sight while forgetting to bring them home to his own family. He had fought in the Civil War because, to him, Abraham Lincoln was a working class hero and proponent of racial equality. As a man who on occasion sponsored or arranged for radical speakers, Michael Higgins was often the center of controversy. When an agnostic was denied the right to speak in a hall owned by a local minister, Margaret's father gave him the opportunity to speak in the woods behind their house. From then on both the father and his family were tarred with the same brush of political radicalism and atheism. It was a characterization that was to cost the family dearly.

Margaret's mother suffered from tuberculosis for years. Her daughter remembered Mrs. Higgins as always being either pregnant or nursing a child. The demands of taking care of so large a family with its attendant responsibilities of cooking, cleaning, laundering, and marketing made further inroads into her health. Poverty aged her prematurely, as it did most of the poor people of Corning, and the Higgins children had to pitch in to help the family function. Aggravating the situation was Michael Higgins' status as persona non grata because of his freethinking radical views, and he could not find work in town. He often had to travel far away for a week at a time to earn his precarious living. Yet Margaret's parents were very devoted to each other, and they faced the ever recurring problems with equanimity. Mr. Higgins was a loving husband and father, often nursing his sick wife or children.

The Higgins' household was, despite poverty and illness, a happy one. While the children were given various responsibilities, ample time was left for athletics, hunting and fishing, and socializing. Mr. Higgins had an attitude towards his children that was for that time an uncommon one. He encouraged his children to think for themselves and to express their own ideas freely instead of being obedient and submissive. He also infused in them the idea that service to mankind should be of paramount importance in their lives, and that they should recognize that all people, regardless of race, sex or religion are, and should be, treated as equals. Freedom of the mind, the body, and the soul were ideals that he constantly hammered home to his children. It was an atmosphere in which ideas and ideals were discussed and practiced as well.

Margaret Higgins began to mature into a fiercely independent, sensitive and perceptive young woman. She rejected the notion of fear or simple compliance and often devised simple tests to challenge her mettle. Once she began going upstairs without a light to her room, something she had previously dreaded. She also leaped from the barn rafters to a haystack more than thirty feet below, and walked the railroad bridge, risking falling between the ties into the river or being struck by an oncoming train. The last escapade nearly proved fatal.

A graphic example of Margaret Higgins' independence was triggered by an incident that occurred in school. Shortly before she was to complete the eighth grade, she came to class a few minutes late. The teacher proceeded to berate and to taunt her in front of the class because of her tardiness. Margaret got up and stalked out of the room. Returning home, she announced to her stunned family that she would never return to that school. The family's pleas were futile and a decision was finally made to scrape together enough money to send Margaret to Claverack College and Hudson River Institute in Hudson, New York, an advanced private school from which the obviously bright young woman would gain a great deal. Here the tightly knit family showed its loyalty and generosity. Mary and Nan, Margaret's older sisters, who were already working, agreed to pay for her tuition, books and clothing. Margaret would have to wait on tables and wash dishes to earn the money for her room and board.

This proved to be the turning point in Margaret Higgins' life. She was exposed to an excellent institution of learning, sympathetic and able teachers, and an opportunity to be self-reliant.

Claverack College opened up her eyes and mind. She met highly intelligent and more worldly peers, and she also experienced the kind of intellectual activity that was conducive to expanding her receptive, keen mind. Because she did not have the spending money necessary to go home frequently or to enjoy weekend or holiday trips, Margaret channeled all her energies into many school activities. She was particularly interested and capable in elocution and dramatics and soon developed a well-earned reputation as a debater. The experience she got at home in the clash of ideas inevitably led Margaret to debating—at Saturday chapel, in her classes or anywhere that the opportunity might arise. The subject that interested her most at the time was the role of women in history and she was soon steeped in research on the lives of famous women such as Helen of Troy, Joan of Arc, Cleopatra, Ruth and many others. It was only natural that she move from the history of women to the rights of women.

When she prepared to present her essay on "Women's Rights" at a Saturday chapel session, she was warned by girls at the school that she would jeopardize her opportunities for marriage, and the young men at the college taunted her. Still, Margaret delivered her talk, and though she failed to convince many of her listeners of the validity of her position, she at least was given a fair hearing. It was a significant event though, since women in those days were for all practical purposes second-class citizens and virtual pieces of property.

Margaret Higgins went her own way many times. She often was the moving force or leader behind violation of school rules and regulations involving walking with young men in prohibited areas or leaving school grounds without permission. Mr. Flack, the principal, came upon Margaret during one of these forbidden forays, but he handled the situation with great discretion and wisdom. From him Miss Higgins learned that she had the gift of leadership, but she needed to control and to direct it properly. It was an insight that was to prove very helpful to her.

After three years at Claverack College Margaret Higgins accepted a first grade teaching position in a Paterson, New Jersey public school. It was a trying and exhausting assignment. The untried teacher had eighty-four foreignborn youngsters in one class. Her budding teaching career was cut short by the critical illness of her mother which forced her to return home.

Margaret tended to her mother whose tuberculosis condition had left her spent and worn. A loving and devoted daughter, she was at her mother's bedside day and night. She studied medical books to learn how to take better care of her mother, but she died despite her ministrations. The family was shattered by the death of the gentle and loving woman.

Margaret's father, crazed with grief, was transformed from a kind and loving person to a raging tyrant. The boys had to go to bed as soon as they had completed their homework, and the girls were discouraged from meeting young men, and Mr. Higgins insisted that they be home no later than 10:00 P.M. The 10:00 P.M. curfew led to a serious split between Margaret and her father. Coming home about three minutes after ten from an open-air concert, Margaret discovered that the door to the house had been locked by her enraged father. Equally strongminded, Margaret spent the night at the house of a friend, refused to return home the following morning, and went on to Elmira, New York where she stayed with friends for about a week. The repeated urgings of her father and her older sisters finally brought her home, but there was a gulf between father and daughter that could not be spanned.

Margaret continued to manage the household with its housekeeping and financial details, but she and Michael Higgins rarely spoke. He resented her reading, her dating and even her ambition to become a doctor, a dream that had been fueled by her mother's illness. Since becoming a doctor was impossible in light of her limited education and finances, ·Margaret Higgins decided to study nursing and in July, 1900 she enrolled in Nurses Training School of White Plains, New York in the face of her father's objections and criticisms.

As a probationer Margaret worked hard and had many responsibilities since in those years there were no residents, internes or paramedical workers. She was by no means perfect though, on one occasion bandaging the wrong leg of a patient. The tremendous pace under which she had to function soon took its toll, and she too developed tuberculosis. Shortly after an operation she was up and about, working the night shift. Her work was difficult and frustrating, but Margaret was happy because she felt she was providing a service to humanity. In the hospital the sensitive probationer also came face to face with the mysteries, wonders and tragedies of the life cycle from birth to death. It was here that her interest in birth control was developed as a result of the frequent requests for information about preventing pregnancy directed to her by mothers in the hospital.

For the last few months of her nurse's training, Margaret Higgins was sent to the Manhattan Eye and Ear Hospital in New York, a common nursing education practice in those days. There she received training in the latest surgical techniques and equipment, but in New York something far more momentous happened.

While attending a dance with one of the hospital's doctors she met his architect, a handsome young man named William Sanger. Though he was a fairly successful architect, his real interest lay in painting and he hoped to go to Paris to live and to paint. Their friendship bloomed and on August 18, 1902 they were married. The first year of marriage was a happy one, but soon problems began to crop up. Margaret Sarger's tuberculosis flared up again, and she soon learned that she was pregnant. Forced to go to Saranac Lake, New York in the Adirondack Mountains to recover, she returned to New York just in time to give birth to her son, Stuart, in October, 1903. Exhausted by the birth of the baby, she was forced to leave the city and to take up residence in a farmhouse near the upstate tuberculosis sanitarium.

The ravages of tuberculosis had drained her energy. Over an eight month period she began to fade to a point where she no longer cared whether she lived or died. With the help of a young doctor and the determination that welled up out of her love for her family, Mrs. Sanger recovered and returned to the suburban life of the wife of a successful architect and ultimately the mother of three children. Despite a comfortable life with a loving and devoted husband and children in a beautiful home in Hastings-on-the-Hudson, New York, Margaret Sanger began to feel the need to do something more with her life and became ever more conscious of the social and political ferment that surrounded them in New York and other major cities of the United States. Soon the Sanger family moved back to New York City.

A tremendous change took place in their lives. They had come from the idyllic and tranquil suburban life of Westchester County into a city embroiled in the problems of unemployment, slums, labor strife and violence. Union organizers, political revolutionaries and their opponents squared off verbally and physically almost daily, and Bill and Margaret Sanger were soon involved in the leading issues of the day.

The family's finances had been depleted as the result of Margaret's illness and the move to New York. To help out Margaret went back to nursing work, specializing in childbirth cases, while Bill's mother took care of the children. Cases poured in after a while and Mrs. Sanger often found herself involved with confinements in the teeming tenements of the lower East Side. There she saw the tremendous gap between life in the suburban splendor of Hastings and the urban blight of overcrowded and unsanitary apartments of the lower East Side.

Actively involved in radical political and intellectual circles of the day, she was deeply moved and disturbed by what she saw, particularly the high infant mortality rate and the despair of women who were constantly bearing and rearing children whom they could not adequately tend to or support.

The components of her destiny were slowly beginning to coalesce. Margaret Sanger had been encouraged by her husband to be more active and express her ideas publicly. Though she had at first shied away from the prospect of public speaking, an opportunity arose which set her on a course that was to affect the entire world.

A friend prevailed upon Margaret Sanger to speak to a group of women at a socialist meeting, and since the original speaker had cancelled his address, Margaret agreed. She spoke to a tiny group of women, but she was quite effective. Soon she was a regularly scheduled speaker for fairly large audiences. The subject of her speeches revolved around her experiences with the tragedies suffered by slum dwelling mothers and details of the human reproductive process.

In her informative and stirring talks Margaret Sanger related to her audiences the tales of desperate women who pleaded with her to give them the knowledge and techniques they needed to prevent conception. She gave whatever meager information she had, but it was not what many women sought—a birth control method that they themselves could use. Desperate women turned to abortions at the hands of charlatans who passed themselves off as doctors; many died from the ravages of too many pregnancies. In her lectures and subsequently in a series of articles in a Socialist newspaper entitled *The Call,* she discussed the reproductive organs, the process of reproduction, social diseases such as syphillis and gonorrhea, the need for education and birth control methods.

Two series of articles in *The Call,* "What Every Mother Should Know" and "What Every Girl Should Know" created a sensation, but they also aroused the ire of the New York Society for the

Suppression of Vice and the Post Office because of the frank manner in which these highly delicate and sensitive matters were discussed and especially because of the terms "syphillis" and "gonorrhea." The Society's strong representations led to the suppression of the last article in the series. This was to be but the beginning of decades of controversy during which Margaret Sanger was the eye of the hurricane.

Her involvement in the political and social surgings of her time had brought her into contact with intellectual activist personalities such as John Reed, who was to make his reputation as the journalist who reported brilliantly on the Russian Revolution, Big Bill Hayward, who was an organizer for the Industrial Workers of the World, Emma Goldman who was an anarchist, and Elizabeth Gurley Flynn who was also an organizer for the International Workers of the World. These contacts led to Margaret Sanger's joining the Socialist Party because she felt that socialism might help to eliminate the slums. Working with Local 5 of the Socialist Party, she became immersed in its activities—attending meetings, studying radical literature and recruiting new members among the working women of the neighborhood and devoting time to their unions, particularly the laundry workers' and housemaids' unions.

A textile workers' strike in Lowell, Massachusetts led to violence and the death of a striker and terrible hardships upon the strikers and their families. Beset by problems of near starvation and no funds, the workers and their plight galvanized the interest and efforts of people throughout the country. Because of her nursing experience and union contacts Margaret Sanger was asked to head a New York relief committee for the Lowell strikers' children who were sent to other cities to be cared for by sympathizers. She quickly set about arranging for feeding, clothing, housing and medically examining them. The arrival of the children in New York electrified the nation, but it angered the textile manufacturers who feared a public relations backlash. Another group of children, set to leave for Philadelphia from

Grand Central Station, was attacked by the police and their parents arrested. The incident led to a Congressional investigation in Washington, D.C. at which Margaret Sanger testified about the desperate lives of the textile workers and their families. Soon after, the strike was settled in favor of the workers, and Margaret Sanger had become a personality on the national scene. She was deeply affected by the plight of the poor and their need for higher wages and better working conditions, but she was obsessed with the obvious link between poverty and large families. To her the heart of the matter lay in birth control and limiting family size.

Margaret Sanger then embarked on a research project of vital importance; namely, all known birth control methods. From her research she learned that most of the birth control methods relied upon the knowledge and control of the man while the two methods involving control on the part of the woman were virtually unknown to the public. Furthermore, there was no sound research to assure the effectiveness of those two methods. Her efforts exhausted her after a while, and her husband and children complained that she was far more involved with her study than she was with them. That summer she and the entire family vacationed together on Cape Cod, but she continued to brood about the birth control problem. One day Bill Haywood, the I.W.W. leader, gave her an idea. She should go to France where women for generations had been limiting the size of their families. There she would probably find the answers she sought. So in 1913 Margaret and Bill Sanger sold their Hastings home and moved to Paris. There Bill would fulfill his dream of painting, and Margaret would search for practical methods of birth control.

In Paris, the Sangers put their plans into action. Margaret Sanger learned that ever since the days of Napoleon when a decree insured that family property was divided equally among all members, small families had become a common practice in France. The small family concept was supported by many labor unions and political parties. Mrs. Sanger also learned that birth control education was a family tradition in France. From doctors, pharmacists, nurses and mid-wives she gleaned the various contraception methods used there. What she had learned about in general terms from books she was getting in practical specific terms from the French. So along with condoms and the withdrawal method she was now familiar with the diaphragm and the pessary devices. Equipped with new information and samples of the various birth control devices used in France, she was now ready to return to the U.S. to put her knowledge to practical use. Bill, however, who was happy with his painting was not ready to return so he agreed that his wife and children should go home without him. It was in effect the end of their twelve year marriage, since for some time they had been drifting apart. Margaret Sanger had chosen to help women even though it cost her her marriage.

Back in New York, Margaret Sanger decided that an organized educational campaign on the subject of birth control was necessary. The medium she chose for her aggressive effort was a new monthly newspaper called the *Woman Rebel.* She served as the publication's editor, publisher, fund raiser and staff and her Manhattan apartment served as its publishing headquarters. In line with its name the new publication called for a women's rebellion against the stereotyped cruel concept of women's role. The newspaper's major policy statement centered around rallying of support for birth control. Circulation grew with the help of labor unions, political parties such as the Socialist Party and various feminist groups. The paper had its supporters and its detractors. No one was a middle roader, particularly the Post Office, which refused to mail the first issue since it was "unmailable." Risking arrest and imprisonment, a possible term of five years and a fine of one thousand dollars, she mailed out issues in open defiance of the Post Office ruling and continued to do so for several months.

Faced with court action, Margaret Sanger carried her defiance one step further. Instead of just advocating support of the principle of birth control she decided to respond to the pleas of many of her readers and provide details of particular birth control methods. She prepared a pamphlet called "Family Limitation" and in it described with accompanying diagrams in a factual, detached tone various birth control devices such as condoms, douches, sponges and diaphragms. This was a direct challenge to the Comstock law on obscenity, but Mrs. Sanger would not be stopped. She found a printer willing to risk the possibility of imprisonment and financial ruin and soon one hundred thousand were prepared secretly. Meanwhile her family had learned of the furor and unsuccessfully tried to dissuade her from her course of action. Inevitably she received notice that she had been indicted on nine counts of violation of the Comstock law. If found guilty of all the charges she faced the prospect of serving fifty-five years in prison. Her frequent court appearances strengthened her resolve to fight the charges even though she was offered opportunities for leniency if she would "cooperate." Her father finally came around to her way of thinking and supported her views. The prospect of prison did not frighten Mrs. Sanger, but to have her work stopped while she was in prison would be tragic. Wracked by doubts and guilt about running away and leaving her friends and family, she decided to flee to England so that she could carry on her work. In 1914 Margaret Sanger returned to Europe but under far different circumstances than those which had brought her there two years before.

While aboard ship Margaret cabled friends to release the 100,000 copies of "Family Limitation," thereby finalizing her exile. Now she had gone beyond a challenge of the Comstock Law; she had openly broken the law and defied the courts. In London she continued her research on the birth control movement in England, trying to determine why America was so far behind in this area. She learned that America's puritannical morality and its enormous immigrant absorption capacity had not provided any kind of public receptivity for birth control information. Changing values and moral standards as well as a desire for a better life style and higher standard of living led to an interest in smaller families. It was during her stay in England that she met Havelock Ellis, the sex education pioneer and author of *Psychology of Sex* and other works, who was to play a major role in her life and upon her thinking. She also visited Holland to learn more about contraception techniques and devices, particularly the diaphragm.

More dramatic events were taking place in New York which were inexorably drawing her home. Her pressing financial problems were minor by comparison with the reports over the widespread dissemination of her pamphlet and the growing furor over its release. Bill Sanger had been arrested for giving a copy of "Family Limitations" to a man who turned out to be Anthony Comstock, the self-appointed nemesis of obscenity and pornography. Bill was jailed for two days before bail could be secured, and at his trial he was sentenced to thirty days in jail after he refused on principle to pay a $150 fine. Margaret Sanger, when she learned of her husband's trial and imprisonment, decided to return home to carry on the battle for birth control information to her own people.

Upon her return to New York in 1915 to face trial, Margaret Sanger was jolted by a double shock. The Natural Birth Control League, which she had led and which eventually came to be known as the Planned Parenthood Federation of America upon whom she had banked for moral and financial support, advised her that they were interested in changing rather than violating the law, and the New York Academy of Medicine delayed a definite response to her appeal for support. Far more staggering was the tragic untimely death of her daughter Peggy, an event which left her bereft and guilt-ridden for the rest of her life.

Peggy's death, coupled with the impending trial, put Mrs. Sanger under tremendous emotional stress, but it also created a tremendous wave of sympathy for America's leading advocate of birth control. Letters of support as well as contributions poured in, and a sympathetic district attorney working with some of Mrs. Sanger's legal advisors and friends offered to get her a suspended sentence if she would just plead guilty. As a matter of principle she refused and insisted that the trial be held. Her decision galvanized international support for her and prominent personages, including authors H. G. Wells and Arnold Bennett, were among the hundreds who signed a letter of support to President Wilson in favor of birth control and free speech. The trial began on January 18, 1916, with hundreds of Mrs. Sanger's supporters and members of the media jamming the courtroom and its environs. Public opinion clearly had swung to her side and the government lawyers sought and received several trial postponements. A month later the government dismissed the case. Though the case had been a legal stalemate, Margaret Sanger had achieved an educational and public relations triumph of major proportions.

She now sought to go beyond the aspect of free speech. What was now needed was a birth control clinic to train and to teach women. Embarking on a national tour in the early months of 1916, she preached the gospel of planned parenthood before many large and enthusiastic audiences. Despite church and police opposition in some cities and her arrest in Portland, Oregon, the tour was a triumph. Her position was being backed editorially in leading newspapers of the nation, and women came to her on the road and at home seeking help and advice. It was a visit from three women from Brownsville, a poverty-stricken area in Brooklyn, that gave her the impetus for her next major breakthrough towards her goal of national enlightenment on the subject of birth control.

In response to the heartfelt pleas of three Brownsville mothers who had four or more children and lived in fear of additional pregnancies, Margaret Sanger opened the first birth control clinic in America in a blighted area of Brooklyn. The two room clinic on Amboy Street was soon ready dispensing birth control information and contraceptive information. Margaret Sanger and her sister Ethel directed the operation. Mrs. Sanger notified the Brooklyn District Attorney's office of her plans and the clinic, completely equipped and staffed, was crowded with over one hundred and forty patients on its first day. Its activities created controversy and sensation. The Jewish community in Brownsville, for example, believed that the birth control movement was a plot to eliminate Jews. (Fifty years later leaders of the black and Puerto Rican community equated birth control and genocide.) After ten days of operation Mrs. Sanger, Ethel and the entire clinic staff were arrested. The subsequent trial was fought as a challenge to the constitutionality of the laws, Section 1142 of the state penal code, which forbade giving any contraceptive information to anyone for any reason. Ethel was sentenced to and served thirty days in the Blackwell Island workhouse. She immediately announced a hunger strike to protest her sentence. Her dramatic action weakened her body, but it also made international headlines. Though steadfast in her refusal to eat, Ethel's objections were overruled by Margaret who feared for her sister's life. At her trial Margaret Sanger was also convicted and sentenced to thirty days in the workhouse, rejecting all suggestions that she compromise. Mrs. Sanger would not obey a law that she could not respect. The actions of the two sisters, who risked their lives and liberty for the ideal of planned parenthood and the right of people to speak freely, electrified the nation. The legal battle continued though, and on January 8, 1918 an Appeals Court judge, while upholding Mrs. Sanger's conviction, redefined the meaning of Section 1145 of the state law so broadly that from then on both men and women could be given birth control information by doctors to prevent disease or poor health. Out of the ashes of defeat Margaret Sanger had snatched an impressive victory for women and for physicians. Planned parenthood had come a long way on the road to respectability. The Brownsville clinic legal challenge would now allow for the widespread establishment of birth control clinics.

By 1917 Margaret Sanger had plunged completely into the activities of the birth control movement. Life was quite difficult for her. Her income was limited and sporadic, and she put the movement ahead of her personal life, devoting her limited spare time to her sons. Most of her efforts were devoted to the *Birth Control Review,* a publication that she was to serve as editor and published until 1928. It was to be the authoritative voice of the planned parenthood movement for years after her departure from the magazine. Her energies were sapped by the need to raise funds, to edit copy and to attract and retain staff, particularly volunteers, and her clashes with some staff members.

1920 was a year of many achievements. Her definitive work, *Woman and the New Race,* was published, and she sailed for Europe once again in pursuit of new and more effective contraception methods. Havelock Ellis had told her of a chemical contraceptive in the form of a jelly which looked particularly promising. Her search led her to various cities in Germany to find a sample for testing. She negotiated the purchase of a contraceptive jelly sample which she brought to the United States so American chemists could improve upon it. The sample was the precursor of a variety of chemical contraceptives that were used widely in this country several decades later. 1920 also marked the legal end of her marriage to Bill Sanger, the decree becoming final in October, 1920.

In 1921 Mrs. Sanger organized the first American Birth Control Conference in New York City. Masses of people came to Town Hall to attend the closing session which dealt with the issue "Birth Control: Is It Moral?" Harold Cox, a gifted orator and member of the British Parliament, was guest speaker, but the meeting was doomed before it started. Yielding to the pressure of Archbishop Hayes, the police closed the meeting and prevented Mr. Cox from being heard or having the issue aired. In the ensuing fracas Mrs. Sanger and several fellow birth control adherents were arrested, though they were subsequently released and the case dismissed. The church and the police were then subjected to a barrage of criticism because of their efforts to curb free speech. Ever ready to take up the cudgels for free speech and birth control, Mrs. Sanger quickly rescheduled the meeting in a larger auditorium where it was held without incident. Still pursuing her demons, she insisted upon taking the matter of the Town Hall meeting to another tribunal. As a result of the enormous publicity and tremendous public pressure, a Police Department investigation was ordered and though the results were inconclusive the country recognized that the birth control movement was not to be denied even by formidable forces such as the church and the police.

Margaret Sanger made her first tour of the Far East in 1922. The teeming millions in the cities of China and Japan inspired her to speak in almost evangelistic tones, and her enthusiasm was matched by the response of both the press and the public. She was internationalizing the birth control movement.

A year later Margaret Sanger recognized the need for further expansion of her activities to promote birth control. Literally thousands of requests for information and assistance came in every month to the Birth Control League from anxiety-ridden mothers from all over the country. Mrs. Sanger felt that now was the time to initiate a clinical research bureau which would be a model for a chain of clinics to be established throughout the nation. The clinics were to serve as part of a health complex designed to meet the total health needs of each community. They would also be laboratory research centers so that birth control research could continue to progress. In order to avoid having the Clinical Research Bureau become a lightning rod for attacks upon the American Birth Control League, the new group was organized with a separate board of directors composed of prominent physicians and scientists. A medical director and staff were hired, and soon the bureau was absorbed in its efforts to study the entire area of sex in marriage, long before the pioneering work done by Dr. Alfred Kinsey at the University of Indiana. It became a study and research center for scholars, scientists, clergymen, doctors, and social workers.

Margaret Sanger's second marriage took place in 1923. After a determined three year courtship on the part of J. Noah Slee, she agreed to marry him after he had accepted an extraordinary set of conditions including her right to pursue her career, keep her name, maintain her own apartment and even to entertain friends separately. Their relationship was an example of opposites attracting. Mr. Slee was a conservative, religious, wealthy, and powerful man in contrast to Margaret Sanger, who was radical, atheistic and impetuous. Their marriage was by no means idyllic; however, it was one based on profound mutual respect. J. Noah Slee was very helpful to the movement from an organizational and financial point of view. This was not the reason for Mrs. Sanger's decision to marry him, contrary to the assumptions of vicious gossips. But she continued to earn her own money and keep to her torrid professional schedule even after they were married.

The pace of Margaret Sanger's achievements began to accelerate. Clinics were set up in Chicago and other cities, and in 1923 she also organized the first International Birth Control Conference in New York City. Hundreds of delegates from some eighteen countries including Britain, China, India and the Soviet Union attended as well as representatives from dozens of colleges and universities and social work agencies. One of the major achievements of the conference was a statement of unqualified support for birth control from Dr. William A. Pusey, the first such endorsement from a leader of the American medical profession. Of even greater significance was the formation of the first international birth control organization by delegates from seven of the participating countries. Mrs. Sanger was unanimously elected president but declined in favor of a renowned scientist. Doctors and scientists in ever increasing numbers were lending their support to the birth control movement. By 1930 there were fifty-five clinics in twenty-three cities throughout the United States. The clinics had come a long way from their modest beginnings in a two room apartment on Amboy Street in Brooklyn.

Mrs. Sanger resigned as president of the American Birth Control League in 1928 as a result of policy differences with its Board of Directors and formed the National Commission for Federal Legislation for Birth Control. She was to serve as its president until 1937 when a United States Circuit Court of Appeals decision ruled that birth control was legal under medical direction and supervision.

The movement's problems were by no means a thing of the past though. In 1929 the Research Bureau was subjected to a police raid during which Dr. Hannah Stone, the bureau's distinguished medical director, was arrested, along with another doctor and three nurses; patients were bullied by the police and confidential records and contraceptive materials were confiscated by the police. The result was a hue and cry from the public. In the subsequent trial, Morris Ernst, the noted civil liberties lawyer, easily proved the validity of the clinics which led to their further expansion. Within a decade their number multiplied some six times.

An international approach to the birth control problem was also pushed. Mrs. Sanger felt that war and overpopulation were intertwined and so she bent her efforts during the 1930's to strengthening and internationalizing the movement. During this period she served as president of the Birth Control International Information Centers in London, and she visited various Asian and European countries including China, Hawaii, India, Japan, Italy and Russia. Dozens of clinics and teaching centers were established throughout the world as a result of her thousands of miles of traveling.

By the later 1930's and the 1940's Mrs. Sanger's efforts reached a pinnacle of success. The American Medical Association endorsed birth control in 1937, and in 1942 the United

States Public Health Service adopted a policy of providing financial assistance for birth control programs in states requesting aid. Various court battles dealt with the rights of physicans to import contraceptives and send them through the mails. The various organizations with which she was associated underwent reorganization and the Birth Control Federation of America, after a merger, was given its present name, the Planned Parenthood Federation of America. She worked on family planning with the wives of migrant farm workers and with farmers' wives in the dustbowl of the Southwest. Margaret Sanger's work and activities continued to maintain the character of a whirlwind.

In 1952, working with other pioneers in the field, Mrs. Sanger formed the International Planned Parenthood Federation. This was another culmination point in her achievement filled life. Planned Parenthood was a world-wide movement and the thirty-eight years Mrs. Sanger devoted to her dream had been dramatic and productive. She had been jailed nine times, fought many court battles and helped others at great personal sacrifice.

During the last decade of her life, despite her failing health and the loneliness which was aggravated by the long separation from her family and the isolation she felt in her constant battles with the establishment, Mrs. Sanger continued to work for the movement. As much as her health allowed she wrote, lectured, engaged in fund raising activities and involved herself in the furor surrounding "the pill," the newest of the contraceptive devices. When she died on September 6, 1966 at the age of eighty-seven, she had achieved in her lifetime the equivalent of several lifetimes of good works.

At her death the Margaret Sanger Research Bureau was working with twenty thousand patients a year, birth control education had been widely accepted and enriched, and family planning had become a major concern of the international community. Hundreds of clinics throughout the country and throughout the world were saving countless women's lives and helping to improve the equality of life in many communities and countries. Margaret

Sanger had once said: "The first right of every child is to be wanted," but even more eloquent as her epitaph was *The New York Times* editorial which described Margaret Sanger as ". . . one of history's great rebels and a monumental figure of the first half of the twentieth century." One can hardly disagree with that assessment in light of her life and her accomplishments.

A CURRENT BIBLIOGRAPHY

Listed below are two series of books. The first includes books about Margaret Sanger while the second lists a sampling of works that she wrote.

Books About Margaret Sanger

Cogney, Virginia. *Margaret Sanger: Rebel with a Cause*. New York: Doubleday and Co., 1969.

Lader, Lawrence. *The Margaret Sanger Story*. New York: Doubleday and Company, Inc., 1955.

Lader, Lawrence and Meltzer, Milton. *Margaret Sanger: Pioneer of Birth Control*. New York: Thomas Y. Crowell Company, 1969.

Sanger, Margaret. *Margaret Sanger: An Autobiography*. New York: W. W. Norton and Co., 1938.

Books and Pamphlets by Margaret Sanger

What Every Mother Should Know. New York: Eugemis Publishing Co., 1916.

Woman and the New Race. New York: Brentano, 1920.

What Every Girl Should Know. New York: Eugemis Publishing Co., 1922.

My Fight for Birth Control. New York: Farrar and Rinehart, 1931.

CHAPTER IV

Pearl S. Buck

"Learning is nothing, without cultivated manner, but when the two are combined in a woman you have one of the most exquisite products of civilization."

Andre Maurois

One of the most popular literary figures in American literature is a woman who spent almost half of her long life in China, a country on a continent thousands of miles from the United States. In that lifetime she earned this country's most highly acclaimed literary award, the Pulitzer Prize, and also the most prestigious form of literary recognition in the world, the Nobel Prize for Literature. That woman, Pearl S. Buck, was almost a household word throughout much of her lifetime because of her prolific literary output, which consisted of some eighty-five published works including several dozen novels, six collections of short stories, fourteen books for children and more than a dozen works of non-fiction. When she was eighty years old some twenty five volumes were awaiting publication. Many of those books were set in China, the land in which she spent so much of her life. Her books and her life served as a bridge between the cultures of the East and the West. As the product of those two cultures she became, as she described herself, "mentally bifocal." Her unique background made her into an unusually interesting and versatile human being. As we examine the life of Pearl

PHOTO BY CLARA E. SIPPRELL

Pearl Buck

Buck we cannot help but be aware that we are in fact meeting three separate people: a wife and mother, an internationally famous writer, and a humanitarian and philanthropist. One cannot really get to know Pearl Buck without learning about each of these components of her life. Though honored in her lifetime with the William Dean Howell Medal of the American Academy of Arts and Letters in addition to the Nobel and Pulitzer Prizes, it is the total human being, not only the famous author, that makes her life a fascinating study.

She was born Pearl Comfort Sydenstricker on June 26, 1892 (to Absalom and Caroline Sydenstricker) in Hillsboro, West Virginia. Both parents had been missionaries in China, but when Pearl's mother became sick they returned to the United States on a one year leave. The Sydenstrickers' life as Presbyterian missionaries in China had been a harsh and demanding one. During their twelve year tour in China, three of their four children had died in infancy of tropical diseases. Within several months after Pearl's birth the missionary couple returned to China with their infant daughter. Reverend and Mrs. Sydenstricker and Pearl set out for a mission in Chinkiang, a city about two hundred miles west off the mouth of the Yangtse River. It was here that Pearl spent the next six years of her life, and the process of her development into an intermediary between the cultures of East and West and the United States and China began to take shape.

The Sydenstricker family adopted a remarkably enlightened attitude to their work. Unlike many foreigners in the political, economic or religious sphere who lived apart from the people in the country to which their work had drawn them, Sydenstricker insisted that his family live among the Chinese people if they were to gain their trust and Christianize them. All of Pearl's friends and schoolmates were Chinese and her parents spoke Chinese and wore native clothing. She was taught English and related subjects by her parents every morning, and in the afternoon a scholar tutored her in the language, customs and subjects of the country in which she lived. According to her own accounts, Pearl learned to speak Chinese before she was able to speak English, and though she came to read and write English before she came to read and write Chinese, almost her entire life revolved around the Chinese community rather than the American or English one. Her Chinese tutor taught her more than just the Chinese language. He also introduced her to Chinese philosophy, history, and art. He alerted her to the imperialism and exploitation of the West and predicted the eventual split between East and West. She played and visited with the Chinese in their homes and felt that she was a part of their lives as much as they were part and parcel of hers. Under the spell of an almost ideal process of cultural assimilation she came to love China and the Chinese people as much as she loved the United States. That love suffered a severe blow though in 1900, when she was eight years old.

The year 1900 marked the beginning of painful revelations to eight year old Pearl Sydenstricker. It was then that she realized that she was different from her yellow-skinned friends and experienced the first painful ravages of prejudice. Suddenly her Chinese friends with whom she had played, studied and eaten stopped talking to her. Pearl's happy and tranquil world began to dissolve around her as the result of political events that were taking place hundreds of miles away.

Those events revolved around a historic occasion known as the Boxer Rebellion. The Boxers were a secret fanatic society who had persuaded the young Chinese Emperor Kwang-Hsii and his mother the Dowager Empress Tzuhsi to drive all foreigners, particularly Europeans, out of the country or to kill them because they were exploiting China. Though Pearl's parents were missionaries and Americans, and they had only worked selflessly to help their Chinese friends, they too were threatened with expulsion or death. Reverend Sydenstricker was reluctant to leave, but finally he decided to send his wife and two daughters, Pearl and Caroline, to Shanghai, considered a safer Chinese city, to live until the danger passed. The family was reunited in Chinkiang a year later after the Boxer Rebellion had been put down by an international military force. The aftereffects of that experience were never forgotten by the young girl.

For the next seven years Pearl's bicultural education continued. She was taught Western studies at the mission school in Chinkiang and Chinese lore by private tutors. At the age of fifteen she was sent to a boarding school in Shanghai. At Miss Jewell's School in Shanghai Pearl's liberal education was expanded substantially. The headmistress of the school arranged for visits to institutions for slave girls who had run away from their masters because of cruel treatment inflicted upon them. Pearl, who spoke Chinese fluently, was able to converse at length with the unfortunate girls, learning about their background and experiences while broadening and deepening her own sympathies. Field visits to an institution which sheltered abandoned white women, who in many instances had turned to prostitution, were also part of these activities. Their purpose was to increase the girl's religious feelings and to impress upon her the importance of doing charitable work. Here Pearl taught sewing, read to the inmates and performed other charitable works. It was an enlightened program now common in many high schools and colleges throughout the United States which carry on a variety of work-study and external education programs. When Pearl went home for the holidays that spring and told her parents about her experiences at Miss Jewell's school, Mrs. Sydenstricker forbade her daughter from returning. Relatively brief though that time at the private school was, Pearl emerged from it with a broader and more profound set of experiences which gave her new insights into the world in which she lived.

At the age of seventeen she continued her education in the United States at Randolph-Macon Women's College in Lynchburg, Virginia where her older brother Clyde lived. It was also a fruitful experience. She wrote stories for the college's monthly magazine and other school publications, collaborated on a class play, and won two literary prizes in her senior year, one for the best short story written by a Randolph-Macon student and the other for the best student poem. With this success, however, came certain adjustment problems because of Pearl's first real encounter with Western culture. Her classmates regarded her as something of a curiosity, and she began to dress and speak more in the Western manner. Within a year though, she had effected a healthy integration of the two cultures in her own life though she was never completely at ease during those college years. Despite this, she was elected to Phi Beta Kappa and was president of her 1914 graduating class.

After she received her degree, Pearl accepted an assistantship in Randolph-Macon's department of psychology and philosophy. She taught psychology for one semester at her alma mater, but had to return to China before the end of the year because of her mother's serious illness.

Mrs. Sydenstricker had contracted a debilitating tropical disease, and of the three surviving children, Pearl was the only one available to tend to her. When she returned to China, Pearl not only nursed her mother, she also taught English to senior high school students and in her spare time studied Chinese literature more intensively than she had in the past. In her mother's absence she also assumed her responsibilities as the moderator of counseling meetings at which Chinese women discussed their personal and health problems. When her mother's health improved Pearl was able to devote herself completely to teaching and to study.

On May 13, 1917, three years after she returned to China, Pearl married John Lossing Buck, an American agricultural expert, formerly of upstate New York, who had been engaged by the Presbyterian Mission Board to train the Chinese in the use of American farming techniques. Pearl's parents did not approve of her choice, but she married John Buck anyway though she had been alone with him only four times before their marriage. In later years she admitted that her parent's judgment in this matter had been better than hers for John Buck according to Pearl was only ". . . a handsome face, and who wanted to live with just a handsome face?" Their marriage was to survive, at least legally, for eighteen years until June, 1935 when Pearl divorced him. She continued to use the name Pearl S. Buck professionally for the rest of her life.

The first five years of their marriage were spent in a small town in North China where Mrs. Buck familiarized herself with the drab life and work of the Chinese peasant—his farming techniques, his daily struggles against disease, drought, famine and personal tribulations. While accompanying her husband on his frequent trips throughout the countryside where he discussed farming methods with the men, she spoke with their wives and children and observed their day to day lives. Few white people had ever lived in this part of North China and Pearl and John Buck were the first whites many of these people had ever seen. The budding author was fascinated by these hardworking, poverty stricken people, and she soon developed a deep and abiding affection for them because, to her, they were the most real and natural people she had ever encountered. They were truly "the salt of the earth" and from them she drew a lifelong love of the Chinese peasant which she carried over into her writing.

In 1921 the Bucks' daughter, Carol, was born and that same year they moved southward to Nanking where John Buck assumed the position of professor of agriculture at the University of Nanking. Pearl Buck accepted a position as a teacher of English literature. This marked the beginning of a ten year period of academic work during which she also taught at Southeastern University and at Chung Yang University. It was also in 1921 that Mrs. Buck's mother died, and after her death her daughter began to write a biography of this missionary wife. The book was to be more than a biography of her mother; it was to become a memorial tribute to her entire family. This biography was actually Pearl S. Buck's first book, but the manuscript was set aside for several years after its completion. After further expansion and revision the book was published in 1936.

Life in Nanking was markedly different from life in the rural country of North China. In Nanking modern Western ideas were beginning to filter through the traditional Chinese way of life and the area was in ferment. Young people, particularly intellectuals and university students, were confused by the clash of ideas and cultures in regard to the traditional patriarchal family system and the highly conservative posture of China. They looked to the West for enlightenment and for sufferance, but they were also aware of the corruption and hypocrisy of Western life as well. It was, however, a fascinating time to be living in China. The effects of change and new ideas were beginning to make some impression upon the monolith that was China in the 1920's.

It was during this period that Pearl Buck decided to commit her impressions of China to writing. Having felt some measure of satisfaction and achievement after she had written her mother's biography, she felt confident enough to embark on a professional writing career. Soon she began sending articles on China to leading American magazines such as *The Nation, Forum* and the *Atlantic Monthly*. It was in the *Atlantic Monthly* that her first article was published in January, 1923. In a piece entitled "In China, Too" she discussed the manifestations of change in China at the time—changes such as the ever increasing popularity of cigarette smoking, parental defiance, fraternization between the sexes, American style dancing and the objections to arranged Chinese marriages. Her fertile imagination and prolific pen were also beginning to work on other literary forms such as the novel and the short story. She wrote extensively and read widely during this time and her lifelong habits of hard work and wide ranging interests and activities were very much in the fore at this time. As a university lecturer, housewife, and mother and writer, she brilliantly discharged a whole array of roles. She was plagued though by a particularly painful personal problem which was about to dictate a radical change in her life.

The Bucks' daughter, Carol, who had been born in 1921, had displayed symptoms of mental retardation for several years. Alarmed about their daughter's condition, the Bucks decided to bring their daughter to the United States for medical treatment in 1925. Much to their deep disappointment and heartbreak, the parents learned that Carol would be mentally handicapped for the rest of her life.

Both husband and wife enrolled in the graduate school at Cornell University for a dual purpose—to develop professionally and to distract themselves from the thought of the dismal prospects for their retarded daughter's future. John Buck had taken a year's leave of absence to study agriculture at Cornell while Pearl took her Master of Arts degree in English literature. While working on her Master's degree at Cornell, Mrs. Buck, desperately in need of money, entered the competition for the most lucrative prize offered by the university. Her essay, "China and the West," won the two hundred dollar Laura Messenger Prize in history. The theme of that essay was to be one of the recurring motifs in her life and in her art. In 1926, having been awarded the Master of Arts degree, Pearl Buck returned to China.

She and her husband also returned with an adopted daughter, born April 6, 1925, the first of nine children that she was to adopt over the years. The baby, found in a small upstate New York State orphanage, was finally approved for adoption by the agency when she was three months old. The adoption agency disapproved of taking the child to China but finally relented. Pearl needed to turn to someone for comfort and love in the face of Carol's retardation and a growing rift in her marriage.

By 1926 she had made a number of contributions to various publications. In addition to the piece that had been printed in the *Atlantic Monthly* in 1923, she had provided short pieces to the children's page of *The Shanghai Mercury* even as a young girl. "Beauty in China" was an essay that was published in *Forum Magazine* in 1927 and in 1926 her first piece of fiction, "A Chinese Woman Speaks," appeared in *Asia Magazine*. After the story appeared, she received an offer from an American publisher to issue the piece in the United States provided that it was expanded into a full-length novel. Miss Buck wrote a short sequel to "A Chinese Woman Speaks" but she felt that the work did not warrant full-length treatment. Her suggestion that the two short stories be issued in a single volume was rejected by several publishers and the two tales languished in her drawer. Unfazed by this setback she contacted several literary agents and publishers on her own. After a number of additional rebuffs she found a literary agent and a publisher who were willing to risk tilting against readers' prejudices against material set in China.

By March, 1927 Pearl Buck had completed the manuscript of a novel and the biography of her mother; however, a Communist revolutionary army attack on Nanking forced her once again to flee for her life. Mr. and Mrs. Buck spent a year in exile in Japan, and when they returned to their home in Nanking in 1928 they found that the manuscript of *The Exile,* her mother's biography, had survived, but the manuscript of the novel had disappeared during the looting. Mrs. Buck took the loss philosophically, asserting that the novel was probably of inferior quality anyway.

It was in 1928 that Pearl Buck realized that she had to sell her writing. Since her daughter was hopelessly retarded, she realized that Carol would need highly specialized care which was very costly. Carol had been brought to a private training school in Vineland, New Jersey where tuition was the then astronomical sum of $1,000 per year. Mrs. Buck desperately needed two years free of the burdens of teaching to write the novel that was eventually to surface as *The Good Earth.* A New York doctor familiar with her plight spoke of the matter to Mrs. John H. Finley who was the wife of the former editor-in-chief of *The New York Times.* Mrs. Finley anonymously loaned Miss Buck the $2,000 that she needed to work on her novel.

Her financial woes having abated somewhat, Mrs. Buck applied herself totally to the publication of her work. On April 10, 1930 *East Wind: West Wind,* the author's suggested two story volume, was published as her first novel. The book tells the story of a young Chinese couple, a wife named Kwei-lan and her physician husband, whose differing views of life—she is bound to ancient Chinese tradition and he is impressed by the modern trends and practices of Western culture—lead to serious conflict. The theme was a compelling one in China during the 1920's and 1930's and the novel was received well enough to go through three printings in less than a year. While *East Wind: West Wind* was more promising than accomplished as a novel, since it suffered from sentimentality and stylistic awkwardness, the work also reflected its author's thorough knowledge of her subject and her fundamental grasp of the narrator's craft. More importantly, it gave Mrs. Buck the necessary self-confidence for her to continue as a professional writer. She had found a market for stories involving Chinese materials, particularly those emphasizing the clash of the cultures of East and West and the old and the new. By now Mrs. Buck had written three full-length books including *East Wind: West Wind,* the biography of her mother and the novel manuscript lost to the revolutionary looters in Nanking, as well as a number of articles and short stories. Her literary apprenticeship over, she began on what was to be her greatest literary accomplishment.

That accomplishment was to take the form of her second novel, *The Good Earth,* which was published on March 2, 1931 when Mrs. Buck was forty years old. It was to become a literary phenomenon, achieving instant critical and financial success. The book became one of the most famous best sellers in American literary history remaining in the ranks of the best seller lists for twenty-one months. It was translated into more than thirty languages. At least seven different translations of the novel were made into the Chinese language alone.

The Good Earth was awarded the 1931 Pulitzer Prize and, in the judgment of most critics, is Mrs. Buck's best work. Into this novel she poured much of her own experiences and knowledge of Chinese life. In essence it is a tribute to the ordinary people who worked the land in China. While it describes the rise of the peasant Wang Lung from poverty and ignorance to affluence, this history of the Chinese peasant family is really a description of the life cycle, beginning as it does with Wang Lung's youth and ending with his death. This book is an affirmation of the author's regard for the Chinese farmers as they struggled against illness, the elements and death in an effort to wrest happiness and meaning from their lives. The book is more than the story of people in China. It is the universal and timeless story of mankind.

Yet the book was controversial and was not without its detractors. Some critics suggested that her portrait of Chinese life was overly selective and at times in questionable taste. Others took exception to her portrayal of Chinese peasant life, believing that farmers were unworthy of being the central figures in a book about China. The objections of many Chinese intellectuals and students of Chinese culture were ultimately proven to be dead wrong. The Chinese peasants were to turn their backs on centuries of tradition and corruption and lend themselves to the ruthless ambitions of the Communist revolutionaries.

The Good Earth was to have traced the fortunes of a Chinese peasant family through the course of one generation. Mrs. Buck had intended to follow Wang Lung's descendants in subsequent works, particularly after they divorced themselves from the land which had been the source of the family's stability and livelihood. Her study of the house of Wang Lung continued in two novels—*Sons,* which was published in 1932, and *A House Divided,* published in 1935. The three works made up the trilogy which was released in 1935 under the title *House of Earth.* The three works in effect mirrored the history of China in the first third of the twentieth century. The latter two were never to achieve the popularity or critical acclaim of their predecessor.

Pearl Buck did not allow her success or the controversy over *The Good Earth* to distract her from her writing. In 1937 her publishers, John Day, issued *All Men Are Brothers,* Mrs. Buck's translation of a classic Chinese novel, and in 1934 she produced *The Mother,* which many critics have described as one of her most unusual and effective books. In this novel the author portrays, with considerable success, the universal mother through her narrative of one mother's life cycle with its never ending round of birth and death and joy and sorrow. In this novel there is a parallel with the life cycle of *The Good Earth,* but in *The Mother* that cycle is presented through the experiences of one person instead of a family as in *The Good Earth* and its companion books.

It was in 1934 that Mrs. Buck decided to take up permanent

residence in the United States because of events which occurred several years earlier. The Bucks originally returned to the United States so that Mr. Buck could resume his studies at Cornell. During this period Mrs. Buck became involved in promotional work on her books, and she often found herself in New York where she met with Richard J. Walsh, president of the John Day Company. That professional relationship flowered into a love affair. Mr. Walsh followed Mrs. Buck to China in 1933 in an effort to persuade her to return to the United States. Those efforts succeeded, for in 1934 Mrs. Buck left her husband and returned to the land of her birth with her adopted daughter.

Both Mrs. Buck and Mr. Walsh, who was also married at the time, secured divorces from their spouses, and on June 11, 1935 they were married in Reno, Nevada. The newlyweds moved into a four hundred acre estate in Bucks County, Pennsylvania which Mrs. Buck had purchased shortly before she had returned to China in 1933.

Mr. Walsh wanted to have more children, but Mrs. Buck demurred. To make up for that, however, the Walshes adopted a number of children. In 1936 they adopted two baby boys and over the course of the next several years they adopted six more children, among them three Americans and a girl whose mother was German and whose father was a black soldier who had served in Germany. Here Mrs. Buck showed her affection and respect for children regardless of their background, and she readily assumed the responsibilities and the heavy financial burdens that her large family imposed upon her.

1936 was a notable year for yet another reason, for it was during this year that two of her major works were published. These were not in the realm of fiction but were biographies of her mother, the missionary's wife, and her missionary father. *The Exile,* the biography of her mother, and *Fighting Angel,* the study of her father, were considered by several Nobel Prize jurors the basis for awarding her the Nobel Prize in Literature in 1938. Many students of literature consider the two biographies classics in their field and among the most impressive ever written. Each biography provides a carefully detailed portrait of an individual of infinite complexity, the analysis of a marriage, and an account of missionary life in China.

Once she settled in the United States, the locale of some of Mrs. Buck's books began to shift from China to her native land. *Now and Forever,* a frivolous and superficial work written for magazine serialization, appeared in 1937. A year later a second novel whose setting was the United States was published. That novel, *This Proud Heart,* deals with the problem of a brilliant and creative woman who wants to continue her career as a sculptor while continuing at the same time to be a wife and mother. The problems raised by those often conflicting roles is presented with great sensitivity. Though written almost four decades ago, the book's theme has considerable currency in light of today's movement toward the emancipation of women.

When Mrs. Buck received the Nobel Prize for Literature in 1938 her satisfaction was tempered by a storm of protest that arose over her selection. Many of her fellow American writers attacked her as did a number of famous critics. Their contention was that Mrs. Buck was too young, that she had not written enough important books, that no woman writer was deserving of the award and even that the award was "political," exemplifying as it did a one-world view of life. There were, however, many who came to her defense, asserting that the biographies alone, or even *The Good Earth* by itself, made her worthy of the Nobel Prize and that her works had a timeless and universal quality that was consistent with the criteria by which winners were selected. One cannot judge Mrs. Buck's Nobel Prize award, as was done all too often after 1938, on the basis of the quality of her work after the 1930's. Like other Nobel Prize laureates her work declined in quality though not in quantity after the award.

As she implied in her Nobel Prize acceptance speech in Stockholm, Mrs. Buck felt that like the Chinese novelist, she had been taught to write on a level acceptable to the common people. More and more she began to actively pursue popularity and a wide audience so she wrote non-fiction articles for the slick popular magazines, children's books and superficial novels. In many respects the most impressive work that she did after receiving the Nobel Prize was in the area of her humanitarian interests.

Non-fictional topics occupied much of Mrs. Buck's attention in the late 1930's and the early 1940's. The range of the subjects that she devoted herself to reads like a present day catalogue of issues of social significance. While predating the Women's Liberation movement, Mrs. Buck spoke out against the stereotyped, medieval view of women as people who must limit their lives to homes and families. She described, well ahead of today's professional feminists, the frustrations of well educated and potentially productive women who were relegated to leading narrow lives as housewives or in positions inferior to their talents and training. The author spoke of the tremendous reservoir of untapped creativity that women represented and the need for society to utilize those energies and skills for the benefit of women and society.

Mrs. Buck also articulated her opposition to war and the need for mankind to take positive action to prevent the use of war as a means of resolving conflict. She felt that wars might well come to an end if women were to assert their influence.

Equal educational opportunities for men and women was another problem to which Mrs. Buck addressed herself on many occasions. Such opportunities, she felt, would serve to reduce the antagonisms between men and women and would also make women much more useful citizens in a democratic society.

Having lived half of her life in another culture, with members of another race as her closest friends and neighbors, Mrs. Buck was eloquent and passionate on the subject of race relations. She constantly decried the often cruel and unjust treatment of blacks in this country and urged equality of opportunity for all people regardless of their race, religion or background. In this regard she objected to the mistreatment of Japanese Americans during World War II.

With the courage and candor that were characteristic of her speeches and her writing, she questioned the leadership of the religious establishment. In light of the abuses, the hypocrisy, the prejudice and the immorality of modern life, she often wondered out loud whether or not the church was capable of providing the moral leadership that the world so desperately needed if it was to emerge from the quagmire in which it was stuck.

Mrs. Buck also argued against the surrender of individual rights and democratic privileges to the government even during the critical war years. She maintained that freedom of speech and other such rights had to be safeguarded if we were to prevent the encroachment of totalitarianism in our country. Her themes were meaningful then. They are perhaps even more significant today.

Her forte as a novelist, however, was not completely overwhelmed by her views on the role of the novelist, as well as her interests in writing non-fiction and in serving as an advocate of various humanitarian causes. In 1939 her novel, *The Patriot,* was published. This book, the first novel that Mrs. Buck wrote after being awarded the Nobel Prize for Literature in 1938, deals with events running from the revolutionary movement in Shanghai in the 1920's to the Sino-Japanese war in the 1930's and the arrival of Chiang Kai-Shak upon the scene during those years. That same year Mrs. Buck's play, *A Flight to China,* was produced, and in 1940, *Other Gods,* subtitled *An American Legend,* appeared. That book deals with the phenomenon of hero worship in American life but has scenes set in China, India and Tibet also. Both novels were more than satisfying in many ways, though not on a par with their creator's earlier works.

In 1941 she assumed the responsibility of founding the East and West Association, an organization which brought artists, entertainers and lecturers from Asia to tour the United States and to demonstrate the culture of their countries. This group had as its primary purpose a desire to bring the cultures of East and West closer together through educational programs of various sorts. Mrs. Buck led the group throughout the war and was in charge of producing much of the organization's educational material. It lasted for some ten years and was dissolved in 1951 because of financial difficulties and other factors. During those ten years in particular, Mrs. Buck argued passionately for freedom from colonial rule and from imperialism for the people of Asia. The age of white supremacy was near its end, and she urged that the people of Asia be granted their independence even before the end of the war. In the same vein she spoke out against race prejudice in America. Given the racial problems that have beset this country during the last two decades and the rebellions that have convulsed all of Asia, Mrs. Buck appears as much a prophet as she does an author.

Though heavily involved in public affairs during the war years, Mrs. Buck did not neglect her writing. In addition to the many radio plays that she wrote, she also produced several books of essays as well as several books for children. During those years she also published a number of her better known novels. *Dragon Seed,* a novel about the Japanese conquest of China and its accompanying inhumanity and cruelty followed by the guerilla warfare engaged in by the populace, appeared in 1942, and *The Promise,* sequel to *Dragon Seed,* which dealt with the Chinese campaign in Burma, was issued in 1943.

Because she wrote with such ease, Mrs. Buck was very prolific and she was able to produce books in relatively short order. Because her publisher-husband felt that no more than one book per year should be issued under her name and because she worried about being too closely identified with China, Mrs. Buck adopted a male *nom de plume* during the 1940's and 1950's. Under the pseudonym John Sedges she published five novels: *The Townsman* (1945), *The Angry Wife* (1947), *The Long*

Love (1949), *Bright Procession* (1952) and *Voices in the House* (1958). Mrs. Buck shed her *nom de plume* officially in 1958 in a public declaration in the preface to the collected edition of three of those novels. All the books have an American setting.

A prodigious worker, Mrs. Buck was writing novels under her own name at the same time that she was producing books under her pseudonym, John Sedges. *Pavillion of Women,* which was published in 1946, was one of her most popular efforts during those years. Using Madame Wu as the central figure of the novel, Mrs. Buck spins the tale of a woman who is the matriarch of an aristocratic family. Although two generations of the family are alluded to in the novel, it is Madame Wu's story of how she discovers love and acceptance of people late in life that provides the main thrust of the novel. The appeal of a woman well along in years, a wife and mother, who finally discovers that her life has been devoid of true love until she falls under the influence of a defrocked priest named Brother Andre, touched a responsive chord in many women readers.

Over the next two decades Mrs. Buck produced an imposing body of fiction and non-fiction. Within it were novels such as *Peony* (1948), *Kinfolk and The Long Love* (1949), *Come, My Beloved* (1953), *Imperial Woman* (1956), *Letter from Peking* (1957), and *The Living Reed* (1963), and children's books such as *The Big Wave* (1948), *One Bright Day* (1950), *Christmas Miniature* (1957), *The Story of Sun Yat Sen* (1953). Non-fiction works that were particularly well received were her moving account of her retarded daughter, Carol, in *The Child Who Never Grew* (1950) and *My Several Worlds* (1954), an autobiography. Mrs. Buck had a facility for writing plays such as *The First Wife* (produced in 1945), *A Desert Incident* (1959), *Christine* (a musical produced in 1960), as well as movie scripts such as *Satan Never Sleeps* (1962), and short story collections such as *Hearts Come Home and Other Stories* (1962), and *Stories of China* (1964). Few writers in the history of literature have been able to match the variety, popularity and volume of her work.

Pearl S. Buck's prodigious literary achievements have certainly earned her a niche in the history of popular American literature; however, her work as a philanthropist and humanitarian have also earned her a place of honor in contemporary American social history. She was a lifelong foe of racial prejudice. She fought against the plague of prejudice long before it had become fashionable or politic to do so. Her entire life straddled two cultures, and she experienced both the satisfactions and the frustrations of being part of an integrated society. It was for this reason that she founded the East and West Association, an organization which brought entertainers and lecturers from Asia to tour the United States to discuss and demonstrate the culture of their countries to people on this continent. The organization functioned for about ten years bringing about an interchange of books, lectures, movies and radio programs and made a more than modest contribution to improving East-West harmony and understanding.

Before and after World War II, she was active in providing China with urgently needed food and medical supplies. As a staunch libertarian she advocated India's independence from England. Mrs. Buck was also one of the founding members of the Mahatma Gandhi Memorial Foundation which was established to promote Gandhi's ideals. Towards the end of that decade, in 1949, Mrs. Buck and her husband-publisher, Richard Walsh, founded Welcome House, a non-profit adoption agency for American-Asian children born to Asian women who had been left behind by American servicemen. It was an agency that emerged as a result of the problem of finding families that were willing to take in these children who were of mixed parentage. There were few homes or agencies available to these children so Welcome House filled a great void. In many cases the children had been abandoned by both their parents and were ostracized in both the Asian country and in America. Recognizing that these young people could become social as well as political problems, Mrs. Buck and her husband began Welcome House by accepting into their own home a Chinese-American infant and an Indian-American baby. Soon sympathetic interested neighbors became involved, and a house was set up nearby where foster parents could take care of these children. Since then Welcome House has tended to and placed hundreds of orphaned and neglected children who have grown up to become responsible and proud Americans with a deep interest in their Asian and American heritage.

Another area in which Mrs. Buck took a keen interest was in programs for mentally retarded children. Since her daughter, Carol, was hopelessly retarded, she was quite prominent in marshalling support for training and research programs for working with the retarded.

Always on the lookout for worthwhile social causes that she might support, Mrs. Buck was also heavily involved in the American scene. She was a member of the national committee of the American Civil Liberties Union and spoke out against the encroachments upon individual civil liberties, book censorship, and the growing influence of the military on American life.

The bulk of Mrs. Buck's energies from 1963 on were devoted to furthering the work of the Pearl S. Buck Foundation of Philadelphia. She had consigned to it a major portion of her royalties. The foundation has been instrumental in helping to effect the adoption of countless numbers of Amerasian children and the creation of foundation centers for children in Japan and Korea. Under the terms of Mrs. Buck's will, a major portion of her estate was given to the foundation.

Pearl S. Buck died on March 6, 1973. At her death her reputation as a literary figure was in serious decline; yet, one cannot deny that in the dozens of books she wrote in different genres, several are acknowledged masterpieces. And, one of the most successful and popular writers of all time, she brought immeasurable pleasure to millions of readers.

If those literary achievements in and of themselves were not enough, she made very significant contributions to bringing about greater understanding among the nations and cultures of the world, to promoting the brotherhood of mankind and to helping thousands of neglected children find homes and love. Hers was a voice that always was raised in favor of the underdog and against prejudice, and hers was a conscience that could not be intimidated. That rare combination of prodigious and often impressive literary output coupled with her inspiring personal humanitarianism, courage, and generosity make her one of the more unique figures in the annals of world literature.

A CURRENT BIBLIOGRAPHY

The bibliography below contains books in two broad areas. The first part is a list of books about Pearl S. Buck. The second contains a sampling of her many published works.

Books About Pearl S. Buck

Harris, Theodore F. *Pearl S. Buck—A Biography.* New York: The John Day Company, 1933.
Doyle, Paul A. *Pearl S. Buck.* New York: Twayne Publishers, Inc., 1965.
Babcock, Merton C. (ed.). *Pearl Buck: The Complete Woman.* New York: Hallmark, 1972.
Spencer, Cornelia. *The Exile's Daughter.* New York: Coward-McCann, 1944.
Walsh, Richard J. *A Biographical Sketch of P. S. Buck.* New York: Reynal and Hitchcock, 1937.

Books by Pearl S. Buck

All of the books listed below were published by The John Day Company of New York. In each of the categories only a sampling of her work has been provided.

NOVELS

The Good Earth (1931)
This Proud Heart (1938)
The Patriot (1939)
Dragon Seed (1942)
Peony (1948)
Imperial Woman (1956)
Letter from Peking (1957)

SHORT STORY COLLECTIONS

Twenty-Seven Stories (1944)
Fourteen Stories (1961)
Stories of China (1964)

BIOGRAPHIES

The Exile (1936)
The Fighting Angel (1936)
The Child Who Never Grew (1950)
My Several Worlds (1954)

BOOKS FOR CHILDREN

Stories for Little Children (1940)
The Big Wave (1948)
The Beech Tree (1955)

ESSAY COLLECTIONS

What America Means to Me (1943)
Friend to Friend (1958)

PLAYS

Flight into China (1939)
The First Wife (1945)
A Desert Incident (1959)

MUSICALS

Christine (1960)

MOVIE SCRIPTS

Satan Never Sleeps (1962)

CHAPTER V

Marie Curie

"A woman's guess is more accurate than a man's certainty."
Rudyard Kipling

Marie Curie was that rare human being who was able to combine modesty with genius, love with productivity and wisdom with knowledge. Throughout her life she was able to strike the delicate balance that allowed her to maintain her integrity both as a wife and mother and as an outstanding research scientist. As a scientist her role was a seminal one that was on a par with that of any scientist in history.

Her discovery, with her husband Pierre Curie, of radium, one of the earth's elements, opened up the area of radioactivity, a new field in science. This led to her winning the Nobel Prize for Physics in 1903 in conjunction with her husband and M. Becquerel. Not content to rest upon her laurels though her place in the history of science was already secure, she continued her work on radioactive substances. This work led to her being awarded the Nobel Prize for Chemistry in 1911, making her the only two time winner of the Nobel Prize and assuring her place among the immortals of science. Subsequently she bore a daughter who also became a Nobel Prize winner. In her lifetime she was to earn many other major scientific awards—eight major science prizes, sixteen medals and decorations and one hundred and three honorary titles. This imposing list takes up some five pages in her biography. How Marie Curie transcended personal sorrows, sex discrimination, and poverty and deprivation to triumph personally and professionally is a story that is as dramatic as any narrative in the annals of fiction.

PHOTO COURTESY DOUBLEDAY AND COMPANY, INC.

Madame Curie

Marie (Marya) Sklodovska was born on November 7, 1867 in Warsaw, Poland to parents who were both teachers. Her father, Vladislav, taught mathematics and physics at a high school in Warsaw, and though he was a highly educated and brilliant man, he was never able to achieve a higher position because of his opposition to efforts to Russianize Poland. Years before, in 1807, Austria, Prussia and Russia had divided Poland among themselves. The part of Poland in which the Sklodovska family lived was under the domination of Russia. Professor Sklodovska resented the requirement that only Russian be spoken in his classroom and in all Polish schools and took strong exception to Russian censorship regulations. His outspoken views not only arrested his career; they also led to his salary being cut and his losing their nice apartment located in the Warsaw school building.

The family misfortunes soon began to multiply. Professor Sklodovska lost his life savings in a bad business investment, and to make ends meet, the family was forced to take student boarders into their apartment. Marie, the youngest of the five children in the family, found out when she was barely out of her infancy that family privacy and tranquility had vanished forever.

Adding to the family burden was family illness and death. Marie's oldest sister, Zosia, and Bronya, the sister closest to her in age, both fell victims to the dread disease typhus. Bronya recovered after a while but Zosia died in January, 1876 when Marie was but eight years old. A year later, Madame Sklodovska, Marie's mother, died of a combination of grief and tuberculosis. The family was never to enjoy a full measure of happiness again.

A series of housekeepers failed to make the household a smooth running or harmonious one. Marie found that her studies provided her with a form of escape. She was a highly conscientious and brilliant student who learned to read at an early age and was capable of memorizing large blocks of material quickly and mastering languages with considerable facility. Serious minded and capable of great concentration, she was an outstanding student throughout her elementary school and high school years. She was graduated from high school on June 12, 1883, when she was fifteen and a half years old. The school recognized her remarkable gifts as a student by awarding her a gold medal as it had done for her sister, Bronya, and her brother, Joseph. Joseph had gone on to medical school at the University of Warsaw after graduation, but women were denied admission to the university. Bronya, herself a fine student, was confined to doing household chores and Marie (Marya) went to work to help supplement Professor Sklodovska's meager salary. At the age of fifteen Marie Sklodovska's life appeared to have reached the dead end so common to all too many brilliant young women, but a combination of perseverance and good fortune allowed the gifted teenaged girl to achieve her destiny.

The winter after her graduation from high school Marie served as a private tutor to children from wealthy families as did Bronya. This particular work was consistent with their background since both their parents were teachers. And even then Professor Sklodovska continued to "teach" his own children in addition to his regular charges, sharing with Marie and Bronya his rich cultural and educational background and exposing them to his vast knowledge and love of science, languages and literature.

Marie found another outlet for her love of teaching and personal intellectual development by her involvement in a young people's free university movement of the day. Comprised of young intellectuals like herself, they devoted themselves to contributing to their embattled country's vitality by conducting group discussions and lectures and holding free classes in subjects forbidden in Polish schools by the Russians. Marie was engaged extensively in these activities as a discussion participant and teacher, and the efforts whetted her appetite for more learning.

Soon, however, she made a personal choice of exceptional generosity that was to curb these particular efforts considerably. While her brother, Joseph, had almost completed his medical studies, her sister, Bronya, who had the same ambitions, was languishing because of sexual discrimination in Poland. Marie agonized over her beloved sister's fate and then came upon a solution. Bronya had saved enough money to go to Paris and study at the Sorbonne University there for one year. Marie decided to seek employment as a governess and to use all her earnings to help Bronya complete the remaining years of her five year medical program. Overriding her sister's strong objections, seventeen year old Marie prevailed upon twenty year old Bronya to accept her offer.

Working as a governess, serving as the resident teacher of the children of the wealthy in Warsaw, Marie gained insights into the often empty and hypocritical lives of the rich. These impressions were to have a profound effect upon her attitude towards material things and ostentation throughout her life. She served in several homes as a governess, and after five years Bronya emerged as a doctor. Adding to both sisters' joy on the occasion of this professional achievement was Bronya's engagement to a doctor named Casimir Dluski. The engaged couple asked that Marie join them in Paris and share an apartment with them after their marriage. Marie, like Bronya some five years before, hesitated about accepting. Her father had retired and needed her to tend to him and she also was still in the throes of a painful love affair with a young man whose younger brothers and sisters she served as a governess. Marie's love for science won out though. Shortly after Bronya and Casimir made their offer to her, twenty-three year old Marie Curie was on her way to Paris to begin a new chapter in her life, that of a student at the Sorbonne University.

In Paris Marie plunged into the life of the university. Though she found the city a fascinating one marked by freedom and individuality, her thirst for learning was such that she would not allow herself time to tour the city's endless array of places of interest and she even begrudged herself an occasional night out to a concert or the theater with her sister and brother-in-law. Marie soon became an object of curiosity at the Sorbonne because she was one of the few women who was specializing in mathematics and physics, and because she was so conscientious a student, and so indifferent to her appearance and to a social life. The lectures at the Faculty of Science at the Sorbonne in- spired and fascinated her, but she found the work rough going because of her limited knowledge of French and her somewhat limited background in mathematics and science.

Soon she took her own one room apartment, one closer to the university and the laboratory, so that she could devote that much more time to her studies. Marie lived in a room furnished with the barest necessities. To conserve money she limited her coal and lamp oil and she skimped on food to preserve her modest financial resources. Despite all of these limits she worked until the early hours of the morning at her studies, undaunted by the room made uncomfortable by limited heat, light, and furniture, and rarely allowing herself enough to eat a nutritious meal. At one point she fainted on the street near the university and was forced to stay with the Dluskis for a week, eating and sleeping regularly, until she had regained her strength.

These sacrifices met with success because in short order Marie Sklodovska became an outstanding science student. The labora- tory had become her home and her castle. In July, 1893, she took her examinations and was ranked first in her class. Though awarded the degree Master in Physics she was not fully satisfied. After spending a short summer holiday visit in Poland with her father, she returned to Paris to work on another degree, this one in mathematics. Fortunately, her brilliance was recognized through a Warsaw scholarship which provided her with a stipend that was sufficient to allow her to continue her studies.

In 1894 Marie began to do original research. Her research which involved a study of the magnetic properties of various types of steel exhiliarated her; however, the only place she could work was in the overcrowded laboratory of her professor. There was not enough space for her and her materials and she was unable to concentrate sufficiently. Trying to resolve her problem she enlisted the aid of several Polish friends. They referred her to a teacher at the School of Physics and Chemistry named Pierre Curie.

Pierre Curie was nine years older than Marie, and he was already an established scientist, having achieved a measure of fame for research in the study of crystals with his older brother Jacques, and for inventing a piece of equipment which could precisely measure small quantities of electricity and electrical currents. While working with crystals Pierre had invented a highly sensitive scale which eventually was called the Curie Scale. His work on the effects of temperature on magnetism led to his discovering a basic rule which came to be known as "Curie's Law." Despite these accomplishments, however, he was better known abroad than he was in his native land and his salary as director of the laboratory at the School of Physics and Chemistry was a very modest one.

Though too embarrassed to bother so eminent a scientist with her relatively minor problem, Marie was anxious to meet him. Through a mutual friend Marie Sklodvska and Pierre Curie met, and though he was unprepossessing in appearance, she was impressed by his qualities of mind and heart. He was a man of few words and ill at ease in the presence of women. Small talk and the social amenities were of no interest to him. At first he was withdrawn and wary when he met Marie, having already suffered through a painful and unhappy love affair. Marie's probing questions about his research work on crystals, however, startled and pleased him. She, too, had no interest in small talk. Soon they were immersed in a discussion of his latest research project. They were quickly attracted to one another by their mutual scientific bent and unpretentious candor. That first meeting fanned a relationship that was to fire a lifelong union.

Marie and Pierre met several times by chance, after that initial contact, at various professional meetings. After a while he asked to be allowed to visit her and they found their friendship becoming a deeper and more meaningful one with each contact. Then Pierre asked Marie to join him on a visit to his parents who lived in a small town near Paris. Pierre's father, a doctor and scientific researcher, and his mother, a warm and domestically oriented woman, took to Marie very quickly and she returned their affection because they were interested in learning, in science, and in people.

That year (1894) Marie Sklodovska earned her Master of Mathematics degree, having ranked second in her class while her personal life took an added dimension. Pierre Curie proposed to her. Marie, though she was attracted to Pierre, declined his offer because she felt that she had to return to Poland where her loyalties lay and where she felt she was most needed. Though Pierre respected her feelings he persisted in his suit, arguing that science was international in character and scope and France had greater opportunities for study and research.

Even when Marie returned to Poland for the summer, Pierre kept up his efforts to win her through a letter writing campaign. He wrote of how much they could accomplish together, of how much she still had to develop, and finally of his readiness to join her in Poland if she would marry him. Pierre's efforts finally met with success. Flattered and touched by Pierre's approach to her, Marie agreed to marry him and on July 26, 1895 they were married in his home town.

Their honeymoon and early years of marriage were happy times though they had little money. Marie and Pierre Curie left on a bicycle trip in the provinces around Paris for their honeymoon. They took little with them aside from their bicycles—a few pieces of clothing and raincoats. Content just to be with each other, they enjoyed the scenic beauty of the environs around Paris, ate light simple meals, and stayed overnight at modest country hotels and inns.

When they returned to Paris they plunged into their scientific work in their tiny three room apartment. Each evening after dinner they worked at the table, Pierre Curie preparing his school lectures on crystallography and electricity and Marie Curie studying for her physics teaching certificate. The young couple worked hard, but they were content for they were joined together by their common bond of deep mutual respect and affection and a shared passion for the wonders of science.

Though Pierre Curie's salary as a professor was a meager one, their intense interest in their work helped them to remain serene. Mr. Curie's teaching and research and Mrs. Curie's studies at the university provided them with a way of life they both found all absorbing and meaningful. They drove themselves unmercifully, allowing themselves only the simple luxury of bicycle trips during the summer as a break from their labor.

When they had been married two years Mrs. Curie published her investigation of the magnetic properties of steel, the research area that had first brought her into contact with her husband. On September 12 of that same year the Curies became the parents of their first child, a girl whom they named Irene. Marie Curie was now faced with the prospect of choosing between her family and her career; however, she refused to make the choice, feeling as she did, that she could be both a capable scientist and a loving, attentive mother. What also helped to firm up her decision was the presence of Pierre Curie's father who had come to live with them after the death of his wife. He volunteered to become a surrogate parent to his granddaughter, easing Marie Curie's decision that much more.

Shortly after the birth of their daughter the Curies began to hear about and to discuss the scientific discovery of a German physics professor named William Roentgen. During the course of his experiments with fluorescence in zinc sulphide he observed that it began to glow even without its being directly exposed to light rays. Professor Roentgen had named his discovery "ex-rays" because, though not rays of light, they simulated rays of light, the "x" representing the unknown qualities of those rays. These x-rays could penetrate solid substances such as hard rubber and wood though they could not go through lead. Since x-rays could also penetrate flesh and be utilized to photograph the internal skeletal structure of the body, their total value to medicine was yet to be tapped, but many scientists were hard at work to determine if similar rays might be produced by other fluorescent substances.

Marie Curie, looking for a topic for her doctoral dissertation, listened to the animated discussion about the subject. She was particularly interested in the work of Henri Becquerel who had been testing the fluorescent qualities of uranium salts and had discovered that by placing a piece of uranium ore on photographic plate covered with black paper, the next day there appeared an impression on the paper as though it had been exposed to light. Incredulous at first, Bequerel had repeated the experiment using uranium that had been kept in darkness for months, only to find again that the impression was there. The obvious conclusion was that there were unseen rays emanating from the uranium which had nothing to do with natural or artificial light. Intrigued by the mystery, Marie decided to learn more about uranium radiation, experimenting on her own at the point where Becquerel stopped. Her search into the secret of those strange rays became the subject of her doctoral thesis.

Several problems faced her as she set out on her mission. First there was the problem of laboratory space which was crucial to her work. Space was finally procured in Pierre Curie's school where Marie Curie used an uncomfortable ground floor office. Here she gathered all the scientific equipment and then set out to work.

To detect and to measure the uranium rays Marie had to first pulverize uranium ores and then place them in an ionization chamber. The process was slow and difficult but she kept at her work. Soon she learned that the intensity of radiation increased with the uranium content of the ores that she used, and it did not change when exposed to heat, light or cold. Her conclusion was that radiation was part of the atomic structure of uranium.

Next Marie Curie sought to check all the known elements of the day to determine if any others had rays similar to those she had found in uranium. This, too, called for painstaking, laborious research, and finally she discovered that one other element, thorium, was radioactive as was uranium.

At times she had to work with elements mixed in with other

minerals. When she ran tests on the uranium ore pitchblende she discovered that pitchblende was four times more radioactive than pure uranium, an odd phenomenon since pitchblende was not as pure as uranium. This was also the case with thorium. Pondering the mystery, Marie Curie came to the conclusion that pitchblende contained an unknown element in addition to uranium. It was obvious that she stood at the threshold of an important scientific discovery. Pierre Curie then decided, in a true and unselfish scientific spirit, to defer his own research on crystals to work with his wife.

The major task that now lay before them was to separate the mysterious new element from the pitchblende. To accomplish this they developed a new procedure based on radioactivity. It required that they first separate the compounds of the pitchblende by the usual chemical analysis and then each of the compounds was measured for radioactivity which became increasingly concentrated in the substances retained. Slowly and surely they separated the pitchblende from the new element. Soon, to their surprise, they found they were in pursuit of two new elements rather than one. The first element they isolated the Curies called polonium in honor of her country, and three months later they announced the discovery of the second new element which they called radium. They characterized radium as an element with enormous radioactivity. Their second discovery was to have tremendous impact not only on the scientific world but on the entire planet.

Their labors in connection with polonium and radium were far from over. Since neither element had ever been seen, and Marie and Pierre Curie could not prove their existence beyond the shadow of a doubt, they set out to prove their viability by using a trial and error method. To proceed with their work they now needed a large supply of minerals and tons of pitchblende for their experiments. But the pitchblende was both costly and available mainly in Austria. With the help of the Academy of Science in Vienna, the Curies were able to obtain bountiful supplies of pitchblende residue through the Austrian government which owned the mines. A second consideration was the ever pressing problem of work space; they needed an office and modern laboratory facilities which were air tight. French government and university sources were not helpful despite the obvious value of the Curies' research, but again the director of Pierre Curie's school came to their aid. He offered them an old, abandoned wooden shack with a poor floor and leaky roof, and devoid of the necessary laboratory equipment. The Curies accepted with gratitude since they had no other offers and soon after they received their first shipment of pitchblende from Austria. In very short order they set about their difficult task.

Marie and Pierre Curie worked together in their ramshackle laboratory for two years separating the pitchblende into all its separate compounds, studying each one for its radioactivity, doing the physical labor necessary to handle the ore and writing up their results in their notebooks. They were undeterred by the dangers of poisonous gases, poor working conditions and difficult climactic conditions. At the end of two years of grinding labor their efforts had still not been capped by success. They had, however, published a number of scientific papers on induced radioactivity produced by radium, the effects of the rays and the electric charges carried by some rays, and the action of a magnetic field on radium rays. Scientists all over the world were following their experiments with great interest.

In the face of all this Pierre Curie was still earning only five hundred francs per month as a lecturer at the School of Physics and Chemistry. He was incapable of engaging in the machinations and the maneuvering that was involved in getting ahead in the academic and scientific world. Their financial situation was becoming increasingly desperate.

Suddenly an exceptional professional offer came their way. In 1900 Pierre Curie was offered a professorship in physics at the University of Geneva in Switzerland at some 10,000 francs per year as well as an allowance for their home, directorship of an excellent laboratory and the services of two assistants. Marie was offered a position in the laboratory as well. There was a hitch to the offer though, because if they moved to Geneva they would have to give up their radium research in Paris. The Curies reluctantly but firmly decided to forego the generous offer and continued with their research project.

Their fortunes took an upward turn anyway. Pierre Curie was given an opportunity to teach physics to medical students in an annex of the Sorbonne. Marie Curie had been granted her teaching certificate and received a position teaching physics at a girls' school in Sevres, a city outside of Paris. While their financial pressures abated somewhat, the Curies paid for it in terms of the sacrifice to their precious research work. Pierre Curie was now handling several jobs and Marie Curie's teaching duties coupled with the travel time involved in getting to and from Sevres added up to a full schedule. They drove themselves to the point of exhaustion just to maintain some sort of contact with their radium charts and tables while carrying out their other obligations.

By the third year of their search for radium, Marie and Pierre Curie decided to divide their work in an effort to speed up their progress, he handling the physics aspect of the problem and she the chemistry part. Her work involved heavy physical labor as she worked with dozens of pounds of material at a time, lifting and transferring liquids and often stirring the boiling substances in the huge vats. She fell ill with pneumonia and for months was confined to her bed, but as soon as she was able she returned to the laboratory. Finally she managed to extract all the radium from the huge piles of ore, and she completed the purification of the radium through fractional crystallization, a process whereby through repeated cycles of dissolution of the crystal phase followed by recrystallization, the radium content became higher. The work was slow and tedious, but there was no other way of proving the existence of radium. Their toil was that much more difficult because they worked virtually all alone with occasional assistance from outsiders such as laboratory helpers and technicians and Pierre Curie's colleagues and students. Despite their solitary and taxing labors they were very happy together.

One evening in 1902, nearly four years after they had embarked on their scientific treasure hunt, Marie and Pierre Curie looked across the shack at each other. Uranium, the hidden element, had finally been unearthed from tons of pitchblende. They had managed to isolate a tenth of a gram of chloride of radium with an estimated atomic weight of 225. Though in quantity it was so slight that it took up but a part of the tip of a teaspoon, it still was among the heaviest of the elements. In daylight it looked like table salt but in the dark it glowed, giving off a strange shimmering light. They had proved that radium did exist!

The results of her labors in radium research had become the subject of her doctoral dissertation and on June 25, 1903 Marie Curie formally applied for her degree from the Sorbonne and was examined on her paper which was entitled "Researches on Radioactive Substances." Her paper was accepted after her oral examination and it was acknowledged as one of the greatest scientific papers in the history of science.

Though Pierre and Marie Curie were exhausted from their many responsibilities and duties they continued to engage in research. Some thirty-two papers emerged as a result of their research and soon radium became the talk of scientists throughout the world.

Radium's fascination for scientists was understandable. It was an element about five million times more radioactive than its equal weight in uranium, another element which shone in the dark. It gave off heat spontaneously, some 250,000 times as hot as the heat produced by the burning of an equivalent amount of coal. Radium could make an impression on photographic plates through black paper and it could penetrate glass, cloth, wood, and human flesh. It could transfer its radioactivity to objects near it, affecting air, dust, clothing and human flesh.

Its dangerous characteristics were soon evident. A grain the size of a pinhead could kill a mouse and human flesh exposed to it was quickly burned. Both Pierre and Marie Curie soon found their fingers full of burns and sores. They deduced that their lesions were the result of exposure to radium, yet neither of them realized the daily risks they had taken in their work.

The Curies also came to the conclusion that if radium could affect healthy tissue it could also destroy unhealthy tissue. They began conducting experiments on animals which indicated that when properly used radium might cure growths, tumors and even the dread disease of cancer.

Scientists all over the world began to follow the line of research that the radium burns had started, and soon fascinating developments were being recorded all over the world. The Curies were besieged by scientists and laboratories throughout the world asking for information about radium. The Curies dutifully replied, feeling as they did, that their knowledge belonged to the world. This was a significant decision since the manufacture of radium was becoming an important by-product of their research and there was the prospect of a fortune to make. Within a few years after its discovery radium was selling for $150,000 per gram. This problem of deciding whether or not to provide commercial sources' requests for information on the processing of radium posed a moral and financial quandary for the Curies. If they kept the information to themselves and patented their knowledge they would become fabulously wealthy, but they decided against that course since hoarding that knowledge would run counter to the ideals and spirit of scientific cooperation. They gave up the opportunity to make their fortune and chose instead to remain true to their ideals.

Honors, though, now did come their way in great abundance. In 1907 Pierre Curie was proposed for the Legion of Honor which he refused because of his innate modesty, and that same year they accepted requests to lecture in London. Several months later they were awarded the prestigious Davy medal which they gave to daughter Irene to use as a toy. On December 10, 1903 they received the highest honor of all, the Nobel Prize in Physics (which they shared with Henri Becquerel) for their discoveries in radioactivity. The prize carried with it a cash award of seventy thousand gold francs which they could accept without compromising their principles. That money they used in a fashion consistent with their altruism. They hired a laboratory assistant to help expedite their research work and sent money to Marie Curie's sister and brother-in-law to help them in their work with a sanitorium. Gifts and loans to family members and their friends were also made with the prize money. They gave little thought to using the money to make their own lives easier, for they simply did not think in those terms.

The Nobel Prize, though it was an honor richly deserved and one in which they took quiet satisfaction, had a disquieting effect on the lives of Marie and Pierre Curie. Reporters from all over the world flocked to their modest home and laboratory seeking to develop their stories. Marie Curie was the first woman to be awarded a Nobel Prize, and she was a kind of curiosity because she had combined her demanding professional work so well with her life as a wife, mother, and homemaker. Pierre Curie's modesty and reserve, which seemed so out of character with the concept of a brilliant scientist, also fascinated the journalists. Their home and laboratory were also beseiged by visitors, masses of mail, and invitations to social functions. Privacy, which had always been a precious commodity, now became more infrequent than ever before. Never having been interested in the social whirl, the Curies found themselves in a never ending battle to retain their solitude and to maintain their simple and unpretentious life style.

Many other satisfying events took place in their lives during this period though. Pierre Curie finally was named a professor of the Faculty of Sciences at the Sorbonne and was also given a laboratory which was staffed by laboratory assistants. Marie Curie was named to head the laboratory. Adding to their joy at this time was the birth of a second daughter, Eve Denise, on December 6, 1904. Several months later they traveled to Stockholm, Sweden to receive the Nobel Prize and Pierre Curie was finally elected a member of the French Academy of Science. Their personal and professional lives had merged beautifully and never had they been happier or more content.

That joy was to be short lived. On April 19, 1906 it rained in Paris. Pierre Curie, carrying a huge umbrella to shield him from the downpour, crossed the street at a busy intersection. Finding himself directly in the path of a horse and wagon rushing down the street, he turned, slipped, and fell on the slippery surface. The horses' hooves missed him but a wagon wheel crushed his skull and he died instantly. With brutal and sudden finality his genius was lost to the world. Marie Curie and her children were bereft of a husband and a father. For them, life would never have the same kind of joy again.

Marie Curie was now at a crossroads. A widow, mother of two young children, and burdened by enormous responsibilities, she struggled with her doubts and reservations about the future. Her energy, ideals and her memories of her husband sustained her during that trying time, and she decided to continue her work and to be both mother and father to her two daughters.

Marie Curie refused the offer of a pension from the French government with the assertion that she was capable of supporting her family. She did accept Pierre Curie's professorship at the Sorbonne, which helped her to maintain her professional status and also provided her with the financial security she required. For the first time in the history of the nation a woman had been awarded a university professorship. In addition to lecturing at the Sorbonne she continued to teach her physics classes at the girls' school in Sevres.

Despite the double teaching load that she had assumed, Marie Curie remained an attentive and loving mother to her children. She had the inner resources that helped her sustain this punishing schedule for many years. She was as creative and resourceful a parent as she was a scientist. Her home was equipped with sports and recreational equipment and she sent the two girls abroad where they developed a variety of athletic skills. With several of her colleagues she helped to develop a progressive teaching program for their children. The lucky young people were exposed to a variety of learning experiences unusual for children so young, activities ranging from lectures in the laboratories and classrooms of the Sorbonne to sessions in the art and music studios of outstanding artists.

Marie Curie was a loving mother and a gifted teacher and scientist, but her skills were not confined to these areas. In 1908 she edited a large volume of Pierre Curie's scientific papers, a book that she entitled *The Works of Pierre Curie*. It was to be her personal monument to her beloved husband and professional collaborator.

Once she had settled into this routine she moved back into the laboratory to do basic research. In 1910 she experimented with an effort to isolate radium metal. In a very complex and delicate process she succeeded in that effort, an operation that proved to be the height of her scientific research. During that same year she also isolated polonium, far more radioactive than radium. These experiments and others won her international recognition once again, and in 1911 she was awarded the Nobel Prize in Chemistry for her success in isolating radium metal. This award marked another first for Marie Curie was the first person ever to be awarded the Nobel Prize twice.

Her well-earned triumphs at this point in her life were by no means without their accompanying heartache. Because she was now a woman alone in a world filled almost entirely by men, she became vulnerable to attacks on her relationships with male professional colleagues. Comments were made about her destructive effect upon the homes of several of these male colleagues and soon these attacks reached such a point that she was nearly driven to madness and suicide. Yet here, too, her indomnitable spirit prevailed and she found refuge in the support of her family, friends and professional work.

In 1913 the Sorbonne and the Pasteur Institute joined forces to contribute two buildings—a radioactivity laboratory to be called the Radium Institute and to be directed by Marie Curie, and a biological research and Curietherapy building. The Institute of Radium, Curie Pavillion, was completed just before the outbreak of World War One in 1914.

Marie Curie made important contributions to the war effort. Though careworn and exhausted by her demanding schedule, she delivered radium from Paris to Bordeaux, did a study of the amount of radiological equipment available throughout France, arranged for the transfer of vitally needed equipment to various military hospitals, and even trained personnel to operate the equipment. The radiological stations that she set up were instrumental in saving countless numbers of lives throughout the war.

Her most outstanding contribution to the war effort was the establishment of a series of mobile radiological stations. She "confiscated" all sorts of vehicles ranging from limousines to trucks and equipped them completely so that each was a radiological station on wheels. Day or night she would accompany one of these mobile units to a field hospital where she would see a series of operations through and then move on to yet another hospital. There was no time to rest for there were tremendous demands on the units and their creator. Marie Curie often had to guide the doctors and surgeons who were unfamiliar with it in their use of x-ray equipment. On the move throughout the war and rarely home, she oversaw the installation of x-ray equipment in two hundred hospitals and twenty mobile radiological units. Often she faced the trials of physical danger, poorly trained assistants, personal discomfort, and constant demands for her services all over France and Belgium, but her spirit and energy were unflagging. When the Armistice was declared on November 11, 1918 she was fifty years old, exhausted and financially depleted; however, she was happy and content for the war was over and she had made a tremendous contribution to saving human life in what had been, up to that time, the bloodiest conflict in the history of the world.

Marie Curie's fame led to more than prizes, interviews and fan mail. In the United States, one of the country's most famous women, Mrs. William Brown Meloney, decided to pay the supreme tribute to Marie Curie, whom she idolized. Learning from Marie during a brief interview with her in Paris that her laboratory had but one gram of radium and that her greatest wish was to have one more, Mrs. Meloney set up the Marie Curie Radium fund to raise the $100,000 needed at that time to purchase a gram. Thousands of American women in all stations and walks of life contributed to the fund and soon the necessary money was raised. Hundreds and thousands of people were then involved in the processing effort to extract the one gram of radium. Marie reluctantly agreed to come to the United States to receive the gram of radium from President Harding at the White House. Her month long tour of the United States was exhausting, but triumphant, as she visited famous colleges and universities and major American cities and was led through a whirlwind of social and ceremonial functions. Though she was tired when the trip was over, she returned to France richer with memories of her reception in America, the scenic wonders of the country, and her precious gram of radium.

Though she was apolitical Marie Curie found herself involved with the work of the League of Nations. In May, 1922 she joined the International Committee on Intellectual Cooperation at the express request of the Council of the League of Nations. Marie did so though she was by nature someone who preferred solitude and privacy. She recognized that the international scientific community, if it joined forces, could exert a positive influence on the course of science and world affairs. Among the activities she was most interested and involved in was establishing a program which would arrange scholarships for promising young scientists.

Concurrent with those interests was Marie's deep feeling for her two daughters. She enjoyed watching them grow up into fine young women and sharing with them the rich experience of ripening into maturity. When Irene told her in 1926 that she was going to be married to Frederic Joliot, a young scientist who worked in the Institute of Radium, her personal joy knew no bounds. In 1935 Irene and Frederic Joliot were to be awarded the Nobel Prize for their work on radioactive artificial isotopes.

Marie Curie continued to be active, involved professionally as Director of the Institute of Radium where she supervised its over-all operation. She wrote and edited hundreds of scientific papers. Her work led her to travels throughout Europe, South America and North America, her travels capped by a visit with President Hoover and a several day stay at the White House. In 1931 Marie Curie returned to her native land to inaugurate the Radium Institute of Warsaw. She had been instrumental in its creation.

By 1934 her health was so poor that she often was confined to her home. Despite that, she continued her productive labors and that year published her major opus, *Radioactivity*. To the very end of her life she continued to report to her laboratory whenever her health permitted it. Her health continued to fail though, and on July 4, 1934 she died. After her death blood tests provided the cause of her demise. Marie Curie had died from the effects of her constant exposure to the deadly rays of radium. She had died as a servant and as a sacrifice to the cause of science.

A CURRENT BIBLIOGRAPHY

Reid, Robert. *Marie Curie*. New York: Saturday Review Press/Dutton, 1974.

McKown, Robin. *Marie Curie*. New York: G. P. Putnam's Sons, 1959.

Curie, Eve. *Madame Curie*. New York: Doubleday, Doran and Company, Inc., 1937. New York: Pocket Books, 1946. (paperback)

Ivisney, Alan. *Marie Curie: Pioneer of the Atomic Age*. New York: Frederick Praeger and Company, 1969.

Bigland, Ieleen. *Madame Curie*. New York: Phillips Publishing Company, 1957.

De Leeuw, Adele. *Marie Curie: Woman of Genius*. New York: Garrard Press, 1970.

CHAPTER VI

Golda Meir—A Woman of Valor

"A woman of valor who will find? Her price is far above that of rubies."

Proverbs

The creation of the State of Israel in 1948 and its twenty-five year struggle for survival is considered one of the greatest historical events of the twentieth century. Among the leaders associated with that highlight have been men such as Chaim Weizman, David Ben Gurion, and Moshe Dayan. One woman has left an indelible mark on the history of that country and has put the lie to the generalization that women are the "weaker sex." Her quiet courage and her extraordinary stamina coupled with remarkable presence and great wisdom have served that embattled country well for more than forty years. During those rich years of great service she has assumed the taxing roles of Ambassador to the Soviet Union, Minister of Labor and Transport, Foreign Minister and then Prime Minister, all the while functioning as a wife, mother, daughter and sister. To each of these roles she has brought the unique qualities that culminated in her being voted in a 1973 Gallup poll this country's most admired woman as well as one of the greatest women in the history of mankind.

Golda Meir, born Golda Mabovitz on May 3, 1898 in Kiev,

Golda Meir

Russia, was exposed to danger and the fear of death at a very early age. While a child of four she watched her parents and neighbors boarding up the windows and doors of their homes to help them withstand a threatened pogrom (massacre) by the Cossacks. The threatened pogrom did not take place, but Golda experienced several other scares and on one occasion was actually victimized when, as a child of seven, she and a friend had their heads banged together by a drunken Russian peasant. She heard drunken Russian peasants shouting "Death to the Jews" and watched them burn, rape, rob and loot Jews, their homes and their businesses. Early in her life Golda learned a painful lesson about the burden of being Jewish in a hostile environment.

In despair her father decided to leave Russia and finally emigrated to Milwaukee, Wisconsin where he became a railroad carpenter. He promised to save up money and send for Mama and her three daughters as soon as possible. While Papa Mabovitz toiled in the U.S. to earn enough money to bring his family over, they lived with Mama's family while she earned money by baking bread and selling it door to door. They moved to a two room apartment next door to the police station where they were often awakened in the middle of the night by the shrieks of prisoners being tortured and beaten. Their lives during this period were further complicated when Golda's sister, Shana, became involved in radical political activity. Yet another complication set in with Shana's falling in love with Sam Korngold who was a fugitive from the Russian secret police because of his political activities. Tensions between Mrs. Mabovitz and Shana increased as their differences over the daughter's secret activities expanded. The fear with which the family lived for three years was eliminated only when Papa Mabovitz finally sent ship tickets for the family to come to America.

The ocean voyage was far from pleasant. It was marked by an illegal exit from the country, uncomfortable travel conditions, the need to give bribes, crowded living quarters, vile food, the theft of their baggage and terrible bouts of seasickness. After fourteen days the ship arrived in Quebec. From there the family was subjected to a long and uncomfortable train ride to Milwaukee.

In Milwaukee the Mabovitz family lived above a grocery store in which Mrs. Mabovitz and Golda toiled to make ends meet.

Golda was often late to school because she had to work in the store, and the principal often argued with Mrs. Mabovitz that it was more important that her daughter, who was an excellent student, get to school on time. In addition, Golda displayed talents as a public speaker and organizer even at the tender age of ten. She earned her own pocket money by giving private English lessons at 10¢ a lesson, the proceeds of which were used to buy textbooks for needy students. Her poetry recitations and her street corner public speeches on political issues also won for her a wide audience in the city. Despite her father's strong objections she continued her activities and, over his demurral, she went on to high school, still intent on becoming a high school teacher. Tensions at home were further heightened by Shana's continued involvement with the politically active young man whom she eventually married. Her parents objected strenuously to the relationship and soon, for reasons of health and peace of mind, Shana moved out of the house and on to Denver. Golda, caught in the crossfire of conflicting emotions and loyalties, soon followed her sister to Denver by leaving home secretly.

In Denver Golda joined the young couple, living with them and joining in the social and intellectual life of the community and enrolling in a local high school. After a quarrel with her sister, Golda moved out and dropped out of school, supporting herself by working in a laundry and then in a department store. The work was hard and the hours long but she was determined to make a go of it. It was during this period that she met and began to frequently date a young man named Moshe Meyerson. He too was poor and idealistic but in all other ways he was unlike Golda. Physically, she was tall and robust while he was short and slight. Personally, she was aggressive and charismatic while Moshe was quiet and reticent. Moshe opened new worlds by introducing Golda to the great literature of the world as well as the most memorable music. Mrs. Mabovitz learned of Golda's terrible situation and pleaded with her to return to Milwaukee. She left Denver engaged to Moshe and returned to a happy reunion in

Milwaukee with her family. At the age of sixteen Golda felt that life was passing her by, so she re-enrolled in high school where she became vice president of her class. She was graduated from high school in 1915 within two years after her return from Denver. After graduation she entered the Milwaukee Normal School to pursue her dream of becoming a teacher.

In 1915 Golda became active in Zionist causes, raising money on behalf of downtrodden Jews in Europe. The persecution of European Jews coupled with signs of Congressional efforts to exclude foreigners from the U.S., including Jews, made Golda examine her life and come to the decision that only Palestine provided the answer for a complete life as a Jew. At the age of 17 she decided to devote her life to the Zionist ideal of emigration to Palestine. Moshe Meyerson, who had recently arrived in Milwaukee, was not very enthusiastic about her decision to emigrate to Palestine. He preferred a quiet and comfortable life in America. Her sisters also tried to discourage her but to no avail. The Balfour Declaration, England's recognition of Palestine as a national Jewish homeland, firmed up her resolve to go to Palestine. She was not to be dissuaded.

Golda and Moshe Meyerson were married in Milwaukee on December 25, 1917. Their marriage vows contained the promise that they would eventually go to Palestine to live. Moshe worked as a sign painter and Golda became increasingly active in the Zionist movement. Soon the couple came to New York to raise passage money for their trip to Palestine and shortly thereafter the Meyersons, Golda's sister and her friend emigrated. The fifty-three day trip aboard the ship was a difficult one what with engine breakdowns, food spoilage, fire and a mutiny. In Naples their baggage disappeared, and they ran out of money. When they finally arrived in Palestine their disappointment was even more painful than the trip. Food was scarce, sanitation primitive and medical care limited. The three families lived together upon their arrival in Tel Aviv in a two room apartment. There was no running water, electricity or refrigeration, and the apartment furnishings were sparse. They marked time in Tel Aviv waiting to be admitted to a kibbutz where they hoped to begin a new life.

When they finally received word of their acceptance at a kibbutz called Merhavia, they were all delighted to be able to actualize their dream of working on a collective agricultural settlement where there was no private property, no need for money and where everything was shared by the entire community and all needs were provided for through the community. Because she was looked upon with some suspicion by her fellow "kibbutzniks," Golda Meyerson worked even harder to prove herself. She worked as a tree planter, kitchen worker, chicken coop supervisor and English tutor. Life on the kibbutz was quite difficult what with the back breaking labor, the danger from Arab snipers' shots, malaria, blazing sun and the bothersome flies, but Golda Meyerson accepted all these trials with courage and pride. Her husband, Moshe Meyerson, was unhappy though, because he had come to Palestine only because of his wife. He found the labor dull and exhausting. Moshe and Golda Meyerson's views were rather far apart but they worked out a compromise. They agreed to remain in Palestine but they would leave the kibbutz.

Golda Meyerson agreed to leave the kibbutz after two and one-half years, years that she looked back upon as among the happiest in her life. The couple first moved to Tel Aviv, where they both found jobs. Within a year Golda Meyerson gave birth to their first child, Menahem. By then the Meyersons were living in Jerusalem and they were once again in sharp disagreement. Moshe Meyerson agreed, albeit reluctantly, to another compromise which involved his wife living on the kibbutz with Menahem on a trial basis. Moshe Meyerson was desperately unhappy and kept writing to Golda begging her to return. Golda Meyerson was in an emotional turmoil because of her guilt feelings, and her concern for her husband, her love for kibbutz life and the Zionist ideal. After six months, torn by her conflicting emotions and persuaded by family and friends, she returned to

Jerusalem. She had made up her mind to try to function and to be satisfied as a housewife and mother.

Life in Jerusalem was difficult. They lived in a shabby two room apartment with scarcely any furniture in it. In 1926 a daughter, Sara, was born to them, and Moshe Meyerson's low wages had to be stretched even further. Golda Meyerson took in laundry, taught at a private school and performed all the chores that were the responsibility of a wife and mother. She was, however, too restless and too ambitious to limit herself to that narrow base of activities. Soon she became active in her own political party, the Labor Party (Mapai), and was given a job as secretary of the Women's Labor Council of Histadrut. She had many tasks to perform in that capacity such as establishing training farms for young women, nurseries and kindergartens for the children of working women. Her work also required of her that she travel to the United States and England as a fund raiser and organizer. In London she came to the attention of David Ben Gurion, later to become the founding father and first Prime Minister of Israel. Her career as a rising political star was now certain, but she again had to face the dilemma of leaving Moshe. In order for her to undergo additional training and gain more experience she was assigned to the U.S. for two years as National Secretary of Pioneer Women. Her assignment was a demanding one for it involved her in the political infighting of American Zionism, in editing the organization's national magazine, in fulfilling speaking engagements all over America, and in never ending fund raising efforts. Her two year stint was highly successful and she returned to Palestine ready to meet the perils and problems there.

From then on Golda Meyerson's career took flight. She became a member of the Executive Committee of the Histadrut, the Palestinian labor organization and in effect the shadow government for the Jewish people of Palestine. She then moved up to the Secretariat and became the organization's most effective trouble shooter. Her philosophy was direct and simple. Histadrut had to serve as an economic force in the country by developing consumers' and producers' cooperatives, construction companies, insurance firms, and medical and loan societies, but it also had set the tone for the people as a moral force in the country. Other responsibilities soon were given to her, among them chairman of the board of directors of the medical services fund for the better part of the Jewish population, member of the Political Department of Histadrut and international representative of Mapai to the World Zionist Organization, and fund raiser for a project to build a seaport at Tel Aviv. The last task was critical because World War II was in the offing and the Jews would need a place of refuge from the persecutions and the atrocities of Hitler throughout Europe. A seaport in Tel Aviv was vital for the refugee reception process.

Conditions for the Jews of Palestine were difficult. The economy was strained, taxes were high, and there was no real governmental structure to organize and to provide necessary services. Golda Meyerson was able to persuade her co-religionists that Palestinian Jewry had to sacrifice and to be self-sufficient so that they could rebuild ruined settlements, contribute towards the rescue operations of European Jewry and fund the defense needs of the Jewish community. Her persuasiveness and determination served to overcome initial resistance to her views. At the same time, Arabs in Palestine rioted and struck because of the political issue of whether Arabs or Jews should gain control of the land. The British, who had charge of the country under League of Nations Mandate, yielded to Arab demands in 1939 by prohibiting sale of land to Jews and by issuing a White Paper which limited Jewish immigration to Palestine to a maximum of seventy-five thousand over the next five years. Golda Meyerson and other Jewish leaders in Palestine were facing a tremendous array of crises under a variety of almost impossible restrictions and handicaps.

The years from 1939–1948, which marked the period from the start of World War II to the establishment of the Jewish state, tested the nettle of Jewish leadership in Palestine. Golda

Meyerson and her colleagues decided to fight the White Paper but a split developed between Dr. Chaim Weizman, the chemist and leader of the World Zionist Organization, and David Ben-Gurion. The former believed that the fight against the White Paper should be waged on the political and diplomatic level while the latter felt that in addition to the use of political tactics the Jews of Palestine must engage in underground warfare against Arab terrorism and the White Paper. Golda supported Ben Gurion's position because she felt that otherwise the Jews of Palestine would be slaughtered in the same ways as the Jews of Europe were being exterminated by the Nazis. She was obsessed with the deaths of hundreds of thousands of Jews in German concentration camps, particularly horrible in the face of the limitations on immigration of Jews to Palestine imposed by the White Paper. Illegal immigration was begun with thousands of Jews packed like sardines into small rickety ships running the British blockade and, under cover of darkness, coming ashore on the Palestinian coastline where members of the Haganah, the Jewish underground army, hid them in villages throughout the country. All too many "illegal" never made it to Palestine. Either they were caught or the ships sank with terrible casualty tolls. Despite the dangers involved, Jews continued to penetrate the blockade throughout World War II. Golda Meyerson was an articulate and courageous spokesman for the "illegals" throughout the war. She asserted that Zionism now had but one major purpose; namely, to rescue the Jews of Europe. Palestine, therefore, had to absorb the "illegals" and had to be established as a Jewish State. Illegal immigration activities were organized more thoroughly and were stepped up considerably. Golda Meyerson carried many heavy responsibilities during that time, serving as head of the Histadrut's Political Department and also working for the Haganah writing propaganda and material for the secret radio station called the Voice of Israel. Personal pressures added to her burdens as she and Moshe Meyerson, unable to reconcile their differences, decided to separate. The two children remained with their mother and Golda Meyerson's marriage never revived. When World War II ended Golda Meyerson was exhausted, but her major struggles still lay ahead of her.

With the war's end Golda Meyerson and other Zionist leaders in Palestine directed their energies to trying to gain admission to Palestine for thousands of Jewish refugees who were in D.P. (displaced persons) camps in various European countries. She testified before an international commission on their behalf. The commission recommended that one hundred thousand refugees be admitted immediately to Palestine and that the White Paper be set aside. The British refused to cooperate and tensions boiled over. Refugees tried to enter the country illegally and when their ships were intercepted, Jews battled with British sailors and tried to jump overboard. In some instances the ships were turned back, the leaky ships often sinking with great losses of life; in others the refugees were interned in Cypress. The Haganah retaliated against the British blockade by trying to blow up British ships and by ambushing British troop columns. Hunger strikes were used as a form of protest as well, and Golda Meyerson joined one hunger strike and was hospitalized for several days afterwards as a consequence of her participation. The British retaliated by raiding Jewish villages and arresting and imprisoning thousands of Jewish men and women. Golda Meyerson barely escaped imprisonment herself. Because one of her colleagues was imprisoned, Golda became in effect the head of the State Department of the shadow Jewish government.

The pressures upon her at this time were considerable. She had to represent Jewish interests in dealings with the British who were determined to break their resistance and to make the Jews give up their arms. She, however, was firm and confident when she had to meet with them; her children, though, were paying the price of having a mother who was so wrapped up and in such demand because of her people's need of her leadership. They accepted the situation, pointing out that though they might have been neglected, "for such a mother, it was worthwhile."

The island of Cyprus had just about become a Jewish colony because thousands of Jewish refugees were interned there, often being captured by the British when they tried to enter the Promised Land illegally. They were jammed into overcrowded detention camps in which living conditions were barely tolerable. Many professionals such as teachers, doctors, nurses and social workers went to Cyprus to help alleviate the refugees' misery. Golda Meyerson, during her visits there, was deeply troubled by the terrible conditions under which these refugees of Nazi concentration camps had to live. She was able to help set up procedures and priorities under the quota which led to the admission of many of the refugees to the land of their dreams. Shortly after the first group of refugees arrived from Cyprus, the United Nations passed a partition resolution for Palestine dividing the country into independent Arab and Jewish States. The Jews were overjoyed, but soon they had to contend with Arab violence directed against them because of the Arabs' bitter disappointment over the resolution.

Arab attacks against the Jews mounted, and despite Golda Meyerson's protests to the British there was little effort on their part to stop the violence. Mrs. Meyerson found herself, during this violent period, involved in rather strange situations including one where she carried guns under her clothing while serving as a gun runner for the Haganah. In contrast to this activity she was sent to the United States on a fund raising mission. She was, as usual, extraordinarily successful, raising some $50,000,000 in two and one-half months during her tour. She traveled modestly to save expenses, driven by the crucial nature of her assignment. Ben Gurion said of her that when the history of Israel was written it would be revealed that a Jewish woman had made its creation possible. With the millions that she had raised, one of the greatest and most ingenious and secretive arms purchase schemes was set into motion. That scheme was a matter of life and death to the embattled Jewish community which was gearing up for a struggle against the Arabs who were attacking them even before the scheduled end of the British Mandate on May 14, 1948. Arab ambushes and massacres kept the Jews in a constant state of alert. During this time Golda Meyerson had the authority to act on Ben Gurion's behalf in embattled Jerusalem should he be unavailable. She was also occupied with an important side activity as a gun runner.

Each new crisis brought out another dimension of her courage and ingenuity. Five Arab nations attacked Israel after she had declared her independence on Friday, May 14, 1948. (Golda Meyerson was one of two women who signed the proclamation of independence.) One of the five attacking nations was Jordan which had tried to remain neutral. Mrs. Meyerson, in one of her most crucial missions, had met secretly with King Abdullah of Jordan to persuade him to remain neutral. Disguised as an Arab peasant woman, she met with the king in his palace but she and the king had been unable to arrive at an agreement. She had risked her life but the effort had failed. Jordan joined in the attack on the new state.

Surrounded by Arab armies, the new state faced the prospect of being stillborn. Israel was attacked from the east, north and south. Jerusalem was cut off from the rest of the country and its seven hundred thousand Jews were confronted with severe hardships as a result of the siege. In the midst of this critical moment, Mrs. Meyerson was asked to return to the U.S. to help raise the additional funds needed by the fledgling nation. Heavy hearted about leaving at that point, but ever mindful of her duty, she left immediately to go on the fund raising tour.

Israel survived the onslaught of the five invading armies. While she was in New York on her fund raising tour, Golda Meyerson was asked by the Israeli Government to accept the post as Israel's first ambassador to Russia. Again, Golda Meyerson was reluctant to accept an assignment which would take her so far away from her country, but again she did accept because of her deep sense of responsibility and love of her country. In Moscow she lived modestly, in sharp contrast to other ambassadors, at times helping with the cooking, cleaning and marketing. Her experiences in the Soviet Union were often deeply moving. When she attended services in a Moscow synagogue on the Jewish New Year some forty thousand Jews surrounded her in an extraordinary display of love for Israel and loyalty to their religion despite the fear of Soviet government reprisals. Her love and compassion for Soviet Jewry was intensified during her tour of duty as Ambassador to the U.S.S.R. It also added to her resolve to help those Soviet Jews who desired to emigrate to Israel. After Israel held its first elections in 1949, Golda Meyerson was offered a cabinet post as Israel's Minister of Labor and Transport.

As Minister of Labor and Transport Mrs. Meyerson had her work cut out for her. She had to create a department which had never existed before. Immigrants from all over the world, penniless and homeless, were entering Israel under the Law of Return which automatically bestowed upon every Jew the right to enter and reside in Israel. Golda Meyerson defined her major role as helping to resettle these Jews and to deal with the key problems of housing and unemployment. She accelerated the construction of temporary and permanent housing units, a massive job that involved her providing workers and companies into greater efforts. No sooner had her efforts begun to make a dent in the problem than a new wave of immigrants came to Israel. From Yemen, Iraq, Morocco and other lands they came pouring in by the hundreds of thousands. Golda Meyerson was not discouraged by the dimensions of the problem and she maintained a blistering pace to keep up with the multiplicity of problems and crises that came her way. She immersed herself in a myriad of details including architecture, engineering, sanitation, roadwork and, as always, tremendous fund raising efforts all over the world. Once she had addressed herself to the various immediate problems that faced her ministry, Mrs. Meyerson turned to long range programs. Soon she submitted to the Israeli Knesset (Parliament) a National Insurance Bill whose purpose was to provide medical and other benefits for the people. Her ministry also developed a code of labor laws for Israel, a Woman's Labor Act which banned exploitation of women workers and protected women from harmful occupations and from dismissal during pregancy or maternity leaves. Vocational education and agricultural programs were developed and expanded and Israeli society was transformed as a result of her creative direction.

In 1956 with Arab guerillas attacking Jewish settlements constantly, a split developed between Prime Minister David Ben Gurion and Foreign Minister Moshe Sharett over the best way to handle the threat. Sharett resigned and Golda Meir (she had Hebraized her name at the request of Ben Gurion) became Foreign Minister, the equivalent of the United States' Secretary of State. She had risen to the second most important post in Israel's government. Very soon after her elevation to this new post she became embroiled in the agonies of a new war to be known as the Sinai Campaign. In a lightning-like strike Israeli forces invaded the Sinai Desert and routed the Egyptian Army. Faced with the accusations of hostile countries at the United Nations, Golda Meir served brilliantly as Israel's UN spokesman. She explained that the Israeli action had been an act of self-defense against armed Arab terrorists and that the Arab refugees were victims of the irresponsibility of their own leaders.

As Israel's Foreign Minister, Golda Meir also stamped this position with her own unique personality and philosophy. She traveled throughout the world establishing a pattern of personal diplomacy rather than relying upon the usual round of diplomatic parties and receptions. She personally visited dozens of countries on various continents and established an Israeli program of cooperation which provided technical assistance of various sorts to many underdeveloped countries in Africa and Asia. Experts in agriculture, fishing, medicine, technology and industry were loaned to these countries to help them develop their resources most effectively.

Golda Meir was by now past the usual retirement age of sixty-five, but circumstances prevented her from taking a well earned rest. The strong-willed and highly temperamental David Ben Gurion resigned as Prime Minister and retired to a kibbutz in Southern Israel from where he often bitterly attacked the government. He was succeeded as Prime Minister by Levi Eshkol who prevailed upon her to remain as Foreign Minister until after the elections. Golda Meir agreed and when Eshkol was elected on his own merits she resigned from government service and gratefully looked forward to a quiet and uneventful retirement with her children and grandchildren.

The retirement was short lived. Within months she responded to the pleas of colleagues and accepted the exacting position of Secretary-General of the Mapai Party. The country was again facing a series of crises including an economic recession and a renewed threat of Arab terrorism and invasion. Arab threats of invasion were not to be taken lightly and, as in the Sinai Campaign of 1956, Israel struck at massed Egyptian troops at the Sinai border on June 4, 1967 and in a lightning thrust that took but six days, completely humiliated the Egyptian Army. The Six Day War, the third in Israel's nineteen year history, left Golda exhausted and she resigned again. Six months later Levi Eshkol died suddenly and the deeply divided leaders of Israel turned to Golda Meir as the only person who could unify all factions in the country to serve as its third Prime Minister. On March 7, 1969, at the age of seventy, plagued by a history of illness and burdened by years of demanding service to her country, she assumed the highest political position her country could offer.

Her advanced years and ailments notwithstanding, Golda Meir set a grueling pace for herself. She lived through domestic and international crises day after day and year after year. She kept the peace among Israel's warring individuals and political groups, continued to strive mightily to effect a lasting mid-East peace, coped with the ever present terrorist attacks, and tried to deal with attacks on planes bound for Israel, rocket barrages against border villages, the hijacking of Israeli bound planes, the mass execution of Jews in Iraq and Syria, and the denial of emigration for Soviet Jewry. Throughout all this she went on state visits to the U.S. and other lands and still accepted requests to speak at fund raising functions.

By 1973 she had faced yet other trials that would torment her for many years. In May, 1972 a group of Japanese terrorists opened fire with sub-machine guns in the Lydda Airport in Tel Aviv killing twenty-three people and wounding more than eighty. This slaughter was followed by the cowardly massacre of twelve Israeli athletes at the 1972 Olympic Games held in Munich, Germany in August, 1972. Terrorist violence then took the form of letter bombs which were sent through the mails to various Israeli embassies all over the world. One such bomb took the life of an Israeli diplomat in London. Throughout all these trials Golda Meir remained a source of courage and inspiration to her people.

October, 1973 marked Israel's and Golda Meir's greatest trial for on the Jewish Day of Atonement, the holiest day of the Jewish year, Egypt and Syria launched a surprise attack as most of Israel's army and people joined in prayer. In a bloody war that went on for several weeks at a staggering cost in fatalities and wounded for Israel, the myth of her invincibility was shattered. Though Israel finally appeared to emerge victorious from the war, months later the nation was steeped in mourning for its dead and wracked by bitterness and internal conflict because of the nation's military unpreparedness. For the first time in all her years of public service, Golda Meir found herself under sharp personal and political attack. So divided was the nation that after new elections were held, she had great difficulty in forming a new government. Badgered by internal political in-fighting and a nation mourning its dead and groaning under the burdens of an economy severely strained by the drawn out war, Golda Meir simultaneously had to concentrate on trying to effect a lasting mid-East peace as she and members of her government worked with the United States and the United Nations, and also on maintaining the unity of the badly divided country. Each day brought new complications to the crisis. Internal divisions resulting from the War of the Day of Judgment prevented her from forming a majority government. She then formed a minority government, the first such government in Israel's history. She had, however, managed to provide her country with some stability in the most politically turbulent period in its history. Her confidence and serenity never wavered and at the age of seventy-five, when many people her age lapse into senility, she continued to discharge her weighty responsibilities with great energy and effectiveness. Virtually each day she had to face another life or death crisis for her nation.

In June, 1974 she retired from active political life, worn by the ravages of years of pressure and crisis that she had been subjected to as the leader of a beleaguered nation. Mrs. Meir also felt that the time had come for a younger leader to assume the mantle of leadership and to help Israel meet the challenges of a new era in Israeli-Arab relations. She still continues to be active though. Her counsel is constantly sought by Israel's leaders and by leading international political figures. Also, Golda Meir is one of the most sought after speakers on college and university campuses and on the lecture tour circuit. Here, too, she actively and effectively promotes Israel's cause as she does in her continuing capacity as a fund raiser for various organizations devoted to promoting the well-being of Israel. At the age of seventy-seven her intellectual powers and emotional and physical energy appear to be limitless. Truly she is a woman of valor.

A CURRENT BIBLIOGRAPHY

Agress, Eliyahu. *Golda Meir: Portrait of a Prime Minister*. New York: Sabra Books, 1969.

Christman, Henry. (ed.). *This Is Our Strength, Selected Papers of Golda Meir*. New York: The Macmillan Company, 1962.

Levin, Meyer. *The Story of Israel.* New York: G. P. Putnam's Sons, 1966.

Mann, Peggy. *Golda: The Life of Israel's Prime Minister.* New York: Coward, McCann, 1972.

Meir, Golda. *My Life.* New York: G. P. Putnam's Sons, 1975.

Morris, Terry. *Shalom, Golda.* New York: Hawthorne Books, 1971.

Noble, Iris. *Israel's Golda Meir: Pioneer to Prime Minister.* New York: Messner, 1972.

Ribalow, Harold U. (ed.). *Fighting Heroes of Israel.* New York: The New American Library, Inc., 1967.

Shenker, Israel and Mary. (eds.). *As Good as Golda.* New York: McCalls, 1970.

CHAPTER VII

Margaret Mead

"Somewhere the gods have made for you
The woman who understands."
Everett Jack Appleton

One of the most distinguished scholars and social scientists of the twentieth century is an anthropologist whose breadth of accomplishments ranges from university and medical school professorships, anthropological field study trips to Samoa, New Guinea and Bali and research studies in contemporary cultures, to membership and leadership in distinguished societies such as the National Institute for Mental Health, the American Association for the Advancement of Science and the American Council for Learned Societies, as well as such rich and rewarding work as the Curator of Ethnology at the American Museum of Natural History and as a writer and television personality. Dr. Margaret Mead's life and career has been marked by a scope and dimension that ranks with the most productive social scientists of our time.

Her formidable intellect was nurtured in an atmosphere of learning and high productivity. Margaret Mead was born in Philadelphia in 1901, the oldest child in a family of four children. Her father was a professor of economics at the Wharton School of Finance of the University of Pennsylvania and her

117

mother was a social scientist. Even her grandparents were noted for their contributions, both having served as high school principals. (Her grandfather was also a school superintendent.) It was a home in which ideas were constantly being examined and

Margaret Mead

generated in an intellectual climate where everyone was expected to participate actively. Margaret Mead's mother served as an inspiration and as a role model for the future anthropologist through her sociological studies of first and second generation immigrants which she pursued even after the birth of her children. Dr. Mead's mother adopted her methodical, yet unorthodox professional techniques to raising her first child. Every event of any import whatsoever from Margaret's first word to her early actions and reactions was recorded in a notebook. Notebook after notebook was filled in this fashion by Mrs. Mead, and when Margaret was ten years old she was trained to do the same sort of observations on her sisters. In this fashion the future anthropologist was given training that she would eventually utilize as she observed and studied various exotic cultures in the South Seas and the various cultural patterns that were to become the subjects of her well-known books.

The combination of marriage and work as a creative union was a fact of life that was very much a part of Margaret Mead's upbringing. Femininity and marriage were not a deterrent to useful careers in the Mead family. Their women always managed both very well with Grandma Mead and Mother Mead engaging actively in professional careers after marriage and motherhood. It was their combination of domestic virtues and intellectual talents that undoubtedly gave Margaret the impetus to fulfill her busy personal and professional life. The women's views on homes and neighborhoods and on the education of children were eventually reflected in the professional life of Margaret Mead.

During the early years of her life Margaret and her family moved frequently, always to a town within commuting distance of the University of Pennsylvania. From the time that she was about six, the family lived in a different house in a different place each year in areas ranging from an apartment house in Philadelphia, and a house in Swarthmore, to a farm in the Buckingham Valley. Mrs. Mead's motives for the moves were mixed, including her desire to be close to the Italians that she was studying, her wish to expose her children to a variety of playmates. These included: the children of professors, coachmen, a Christian Scientist and high society families, and also her efforts to find good schools for her children. The Mead children met and mixed easily with a wide variety of people and learned to adjust to different situations. Here, too, young Margaret Mead was being given basic training for her future work.

Margaret Mead's schooling during her elementary school years was irregular, but effective. It was supplemented by Grandmother Mead's tutelage at home as well as by a series of "lessons" arranged by Mrs. Mead. The Mead family had its own progressive ideas about education, ideas which were far ahead of their time. For example, when a severe case of whooping cough kept ten year old Margaret out of school for two years, she was tutored by her parents and grandmother, and their teaching was of such quality that she was able not only to keep up with her peers but to surpass them. Her grandmother had very advanced ideas and taught Margaret algebra before she had mastered spelling. The older woman also was instrumental in training her granddaughter to observe human nature and behavior systematically by starting her off on studying her younger sisters. Mrs. Mead provided "lessons" for her children wherever they lived by utilizing the local talents and skills of various artisans to teach them woodcarving, basketweaving, drawing, carpentry, folk dancing and music, sewing and painting. These skills not only enriched Margaret's educational program; they also were to be invaluable when she lived with primitive groups on Pacific islands when she was a field research anthropologist.

This fascinating but decidedly informal educational process was changed when she was eleven years old. In 1911 she was sent to the Buckingham Friends' School which was attended by pupils ranging in age from ten to twenty. After she was graduated in the spring of 1915 in a class of four she went on to a local public high school two miles from the farm on which she lived.

The following winter the Mead family moved to Doylestown, Pennsylvania where Margaret attended a good small-town high school for two years. During those two years at Doylestown her precocity and brilliance came to the fore with some frequency. Margaret helped to start the school newspaper there and did some writing for the local newspaper, and she also began to see the discrepancies between life in her home and the books that she read and that of the world outside. During the last Christmas before the end of World War I, Margaret became secretly engaged to a young man named Luther Cressman, four years her senior and in his final year at Pennsylvania State College.

In the fall of 1918 the Mead family moved once again, this time to New Hope, Pennsylvania where Margaret was enrolled in the Holmquist School, a new and very special private school for girls. It had a total of thirteen pupils and five teachers and was set in the midst of a famous old artist's colony. An added attraction was the attendance of Margaret's two younger sisters, Elizabeth and Priscilla, who had never gone to a regular school before, at its children's section. During that final year of high school, Margaret told her parents of her secret engagement and so, at the age of seventeen, she was engaged to be married, was graduated from high school, and was admitted to De Pauw University, her father's Alma Mater.

As is all too often the case, the choice of college was an unfortunate one for Margaret Mead. She had entered De Pauw in 1919 because it was the only way her father could be persuaded to allow her to attend college since he had suffered serious financial reverses. Margaret entered with the expectation of being challenged and enriched intellectually. Instead, the students were for the most part the first of their families to attend college and more interested in fraternity and sorority life and the school's athletic exploits than they were in learning. So, at the end of her first year at De Pauw, Margaret Mead persuaded her father to allow her to transfer to Barnard College in New York. Given her family background and her already high level of scholarship, it was almost inevitable that Miss Mead would have to change schools.

The transfer was a happy one. Barnard was a college in the university atmosphere of Columbia University and it was also set in the exciting life style of New York City. Miss Mead thrived on the courses that she took and the friendships that she developed at college, and she was enormously attracted by the city's cultural treasures including its museums, concert halls and Broadway theatres.

The question of what her major should be and what she should do with her life after college was on Miss Mead's mind almost from her first days at the college. At DePauw she had entered with the intention of becoming a writer, and when she transferred to Barnard she continued to major in English. When she recognized that she would not be a great writer, Miss Mead sought another channel for her talents. When she entered her senior year at Barnard she was a psychology major, but a course on the psychological aspects of culture given by William Fielding Ogburn and a course in anthropology offered by Franz Boas sharpened and refined her future interests and plans.

Anthropology, whose principles she had already absorbed to some degree as a result of her mother's use of them in her studies of Italians, was taking an increasingly firm hold on her intellectual curiosity. Through her study of anthropology with the legendary Franz Boas and the development of a close relationship with Ruth Benedict, his teaching assistant, Margaret Mead came to recognize the importance of anthropology as a discipline and as a science. Anthropology was a science that studied man through an examination of primitive people who lived in a culture untouched by modern day civilization. If, through close study of these people, certain truths could be derived about them, considerable light might be shed on human behavior and problems in general. The warp and woof of common patterns in human behavior throughout the ages might then become more apparent, the comparison between ancient and modern civilizations having been made. To gain the most exhaustive knowledge of these primitive cultures, anthropologists had to live intimately within the group for long periods of time.

The friendship between Ruth Benedict and Margaret Mead was to last a lifetime, until Mrs. Benedict's death in 1948. The two women drew upon each other for both personal and professional support. When she was graduated from Barnard in the spring of 1923, Margaret Mead already had many plans. She was to be married the following fall and was committed to taking her master's degree in psychology and completing the work for it during the coming summer. She had also accepted an economics and sociology assistantship with Professor Ogburn for that fall and at the same time she was also to begin graduate work in anthropology.

Margaret Mead was married in September, 1923 to Luther Cressman and she presaged the future Women's Liberation movement by deciding to keep her own name, a decision which received considerable attention. Margaret Mead and Luther Cressman settled down to a marriage that was filled with their studies and professional and social activities. He had a graduate fellowship and a part-time pastorate in an East New York church. She in turn served as a graduate assistant to Professor Ogburn in the Barnard Department of Economics of Sociology and as his editorial assistant on the *Journal of the American Statistical Association* and was also preparing to take a Ph.D. in anthropology while completing her Master's thesis in psychology. The brilliant and versatile young woman was also still writing her highly personal short stories and poems. Those first two years of marriage were pleasant and productive.

At the end of the summer of 1924 Margaret Mead attended a meeting of the British Association for the Advancement of Science in Toronto, Canada where she was highly impressed by the intellectual power of her colleagues. That meeting convinced her that she wanted to do field work in anthropology as soon as she had received her degree. Luther Cressman was quite understanding about his wife's desire although it meant they would be separated for long periods of time. He proposed an arrangement where he would pursue his studies more actively so that his wife could do field work. Both would apply for travel fellowships that would make his studies and her field trips possible.

At the suggestion of Professor Franz Boas Margaret Mead

agreed to a study of adolescence, particularly the adolescent girl, to determine the extent to which the emotional turmoil that so often was associated with that age group depended upon the attitudes of a particular culture and the degree to which that adolescent behavior pattern was inherent in the psychological development of adolescents all over the world. If she were able to prove similarities or differences scientifically, a whole new array of facts about human behavior could be derived by social scientists to help them build a better world more intelligently.

The young graduate assistant decided that she wanted to do her field studies in Polynesia though Professor Boas wanted her to study the American Indian. He felt that going to Polynesia would expose her to danger, but she finally persuaded him that her choice was the more desirable and logical one. Miss Mead then applied in 1925 for a fellowship for work in Samoa from the National Research Council. The fellowship did not include traveling expenses, but her father agreed to pay for them since the work his daughter was planning was in keeping with his personal philosophy that adding to the sum total of human knowledge in the world was the most valuable contribution one could make.

That spring and summer were busy for the young couple. Margaret Mead and Luther Cressman both completed their theses and then prepared to leave on their fellowships that autumn. They spent a last vacation together, then Luther Cressman sailed for Europe and Margaret set out for Samoa.

Margaret Mead had set out on a venture that was quite demanding. For one, she had received no formal training in field work. Professor Boas' courses were essentially theoretical rather than practical. When she arrived in Samoa she stayed in a hotel and was assigned as a tutor, for an hour each day, a Samoan nurse who spoke English well. She also devoted seven hours a day to memorizing vocabulary in the Samoan languages. She stayed in the port to learn the language and then sailed for Tau, the distant island where she lived with an American naval family.

The first of the Samoan homes in which she stayed was in the household of a native chief and the chief's daughter was her constant companion. Margaret Mead was actually living the life of an adolescent Samoan girl, learning their etiquette, sleeping on mats in the huts, eating native food, learning their language, wearing native garb, and learning to perform rituals important to Samoan adolescents. Her stay in the two other villages was equally fascinating and productive as she observed, studied and recorded the Samoan culture as it unfolded before her.

That nine month stay in Samoa led to the production of a remarkable set of achievements. Margaret Mead was one of the first anthropologist to live in the culture that she was studying and to get to know its people so intimately. Her training at Columbia in the skills of interrogation and observation was most useful. The young anthropologist had also initiated a new information gathering and interpreting system which was to be the pace setter for succeeding generations of anthropologists. From that field trip also emerged, based upon the copious and exhaustive records that she kept, a book entitled *Coming of Age in Samoa* which, as soon as it was published in 1928, became one of the most widely read best selling books of its kind in the history of the world, appealing as it does to both anthropologists and laymen.

Coming of Age in Samoa posited to its readers the central thesis that the traits that Western civilization has often accepted as "human nature," are ofttimes actually the result of an individual's cultural environment and his training. According to Miss Mead, adolescence in Samoa was not a period characterized by stress and conflict, but rather one of orderly maturation and transition to adult life. In Samoa there was no evidence of the generational conflict between young and old that was characteristic of adolescence and post-adolescence in the Western world.

In the summer of 1926 Margaret Mead left Samoa on a six week ocean voyage to Europe on the way back to the United

States. Aboard a ship leaving from Sydney, Australia to England she met a young New Zealand psychologist named Reo Fortune who was on his way to England, having just won a two year fellowship to Cambridge as a prize for an essay on dreams. Their common interests in anthropology and psychology drew them together and by the end of the voyage the two were deeply in love though Margaret Mead was still married to Luther Cressman.

Upon her return to the United States Miss Mead received an appointment as Assistant Curator of Ethnology at the American Museum of Natural History. Luther Cressman was teaching anthropology and Margaret Mead often served as a resource person for his lectures, but they were drifting apart and found that they had little in common. She applied for a fellowship from the Social Science Research Council to study the younger children of the water-dwelling Manu tribe in the Admiralty Islands in New Guinea. She had become interested in the problem of what primitive children were like and how the primitive adults resembled modern day children in their thinking. (That interest was linked to a personal motivation as well since she had been awarded a second research grant in that area.) Working in the museum, writing several professional monographs and preparing the final proofs of *Coming of Age in Samoa,* Margaret Mead's life was further complicated by her need to arrange for her divorce from Luther Cressman, and to obtain a leave from her museum post so that she could embark on her second field study.

While away on the field study of the Manu, Margaret Mead became a best selling author, something she learned only upon her return from the Admiralty Islands. Enroute to that second field trip in 1928 Margaret Mead and Reo Fortune were married in Auckland, New Zealand. The newlyweds went to work among the Manus people of the Admiralty Islands because this was an area where no modern ethnographers had ever done research before. Margaret Mead hoped to expand her anthropological experience to become a more effective and valuable museum curator and also to learn how primitive adults, whose thinking had been likened to that of civilized children, differed from primitive children.

The Manus people inhabited vaulted thatched huts set on stilts above the water, and they lived virtually without any contacts with the outside world and so had preserved their culture for centuries. Theirs was a fishing economy and their lives moved in monthly cycles while they waited for the fish to come over the reef when their activities would accelerate. Their child rearing techniques differed markedly from those of the Samoans where children had clearly defined responsibilities.

The Manus children were taught to manage canoes at a tender age but they were not taught respect for their elders or self-control over their tempers or tongues. Children were not given any responsibilities, and they were permitted to follow their own whims or to play all day long. Miss Mead saw a parallel between the permissive, free and easy approach of the Manus to their children that was so true of progressive educational theories. She inferred that children who are given unrestricted freedom do not necessarily prove to be creative or imaginative, and she felt that Manus children's lives were dull and uninteresting. Dr. Mead also observed that though Manus children were never given formal training for adult life they turned into typical Manus adults anyway. It was environment rather than early formal education then that determined Manus development. The Manus adults were hard driving, materialistic and puritannical people who related to each other only because they had something to give to or do for each other. Dr. Mead described their social patterns as a "utilitarian relationship." The children were quite lovable, a far cry from what they would become as adults.

The husband and wife anthropological team found life quite hard during this field trip. Food was limited in amount, variety and delectability. Bouts of malaria laid them low on several occasions and housing accommodations were far from comfortable.

Despite these drawbacks, Margaret Mead and Reo Fortune

derived great professional pleasure from their work. They began to perfect a method that they later called event analysis which was a technique involving organizing insights around the most significant events in the village. They observed and recorded tremendous masses of material, all of which ultimately had to be sorted and collated and by June, 1929, after six months in Manus, the two anthropologists were pretty much pleased with what they had amassed. From their trip emerged Reo Fortune's book *Manus Religion* and Margaret Mead's *Growing Up in New Guinea* and *Kinship in the Admiralty Islands*. In these projects, Margaret and Reo complemented each other's talents and efforts.

There were, however, many signs of strain developing between them, in no small measure the result of her fame and brilliance. She was famous whereas he was unknown, and while he resented watching her engage in mundane housewife's activities such as marketing, house cleaning and cooking, he was unwilling to undertake any of these responsibilities himself. Margaret Mead, long before the days of Women's Liberation was willing to defer to Reo's resentment of the social and practical activities in which women had to engage, but she would not curb her criticisms nor would she defer to him intellectually. She refused to pander to his male sensibilities all the time.

A brief joint field trip to study American Indian women in a Omaha, Nebraska reservation compounded their frustration. The fierce shimmering heat of Nebraska and the culturally as-similated Plains Indians who were uncommunicative and money oriented made for a devastating experience even though it was to be but a three month study. Despite that thoroughly unrewarding experience, the two were convinced that the best situation for them was to do field work together, especially since Margaret had been told she could not have children. They then planned to re-turn to New Guinea and in December, 1931 the couple came to the Arapesh.

During the two year period from 1931 to 1933 Reo Fortune and Margaret Mead did field work which was to give her new perspectives into the nature of sex roles in culture and also to help her discern the various interrelationships of culture and temperament. When she returned to New Guinea, Margaret Mead sought to define the manner in which a culture stereotypes the roles of men and women. This problem had to be resolved before one could examine the fundamental question of the biological differences between men and women that are sex linked and their effects on the roles and behavior of the two sexes in any given society.

The professional team went up into the mountains on slippery, dangerous slopes and across deep rivers to reach their destination. Among the Arapesh, Dr. Mead learned, both men and women were expected to be tender and solicitous to children. Men were very much involved in the process of raising children. Aggressive behavior was frowned upon in both sexes. The male role in the Arapesh culture stood in sharp contrast to his common posture in Western civilization. In August, 1932 the two left the Arapesh without a satisfactory solution to their problem.

Margaret Mead, through the medium of the latest field trip and her earlier ones as well, had created a new kind of field work. She had learned how to study the rearing of children within the framework of a total culture, thereby giving a more dynamic and fully dimensioned portrait of that culture. The method of event analysis, which they had invented, had taught them how to place each particular event within a total framework.

A field trip up the Sepik River followed where they observed the Mandugumor people, a fierce group of cannibals, but the trip there was also disappointing because the culture was disintegrating and all ceremonial life was coming to an end. This break with the past was unfortunate for the team of anthropologists but they went to work anyway.

The Mundugumor contrasted sharply with the Arapesh. Men and women were expected to be fierce, possessive and sexually aggressive, and the two sexes rejected children. The adults preferred children of the opposite sex and babies of the wrong sex were hurled into the river while still alive. Little boys were used as hostages during temporary alliances between villages. In December, 1933 Reo Fortune and Margaret Mead left the Mundugumor, glad to leave a culture that was full of economic and sexual rivalries, exploitation, suicide and violence. It was during this two year tour of New Guinea that Margaret Mead met Gregory Bateson, an English anthropologist who was to become her third husband.

Following their work with the Arapesh and Mundugumor, Margaret Mead and Reo Fortune met Gregory Bateson, also doing field work on the Sepik River studying the Tchambuli people who lived on Chamberi Lake, reputedly the most beautiful in all New Guinea. They settled in a Tchambuli village, living in native houses, and began an intensive effort to learn their third new language in a span of two years. Among the Tchambuli Dr. Mead learned something about the central problem in which she was most absorbed—the culturally assigned roles of the two sexes. In this culture the relations and roles of men and women were the reverse of those in Western cultures. Tchambuli women were the more vigorous and business and group work oriented. Young girls were looked upon as the human resources potential of the future, and they manifested a more alert, curious and intelligent approach to life, whereas the young boys engaged in the highly individual and competitive life of the men. Warfare was a phenomenon which no longer interested Tchambuli men. Though the men were nominally the heads of the households it was actually the women who handled all of the family affairs, the latter acting like and dressing in the simple, unpretentious style associated with men in our culture. Men engaged in carving and painting and gossip and involved themselves in emotional scenes, traits that Westerners associate with women.

Gregory Bateson described similar behavior patterns in the neighboring Iatmul villages where he worked. The trio of anthropologists discussed the implications of their findings on the relationship between sex and temperament. Their primary aim was to arrive at a new concept of culturally expected behavior based upon the differences between the Arapesh, Iatmul, Mundugumor and Tchambuli cultures. They were moving towards a way of describing in organized fashion the different temperamental types that were standardized by the structure of particular cultures. By linking cultural differences to the temperamental types emphasized in each culture, they hoped to work out patterns by which cultures and temperamental types could be matched. Cultures were defined and related to the culture's expectations of male and female personalities. They theorized that the heart of human behavior matter lay not in biological differences between the sexes, but on cultural expectations by which each sex was assigned to only one temperament. Inferences were drawn regarding the inevitable clashes between the sexes that erupt when the inborn temperaments of individuals clash with cultural expectations. They were to all intents and purposes stripping away the cultural determinism that had been imposed upon the behavior of the two sexes though they were also wary of publicizing the idea that there are inborn differences between people.

The work that Margaret Mead completed on that field trip in 1933 ultimately led to the publication of another major work, *Sex and Temperament,* which was published in 1935. In that seminal work and in *Male and Female,* written in 1949, she described the ways in which the behavior of the two sexes was culturally determined in Arapesh, Mundugumor and Tchambuli. The book was hailed by feminists of the day, but its author was attacked by traditionalists.

The last trip to New Guinea had affected Margaret Mead personally as well as professionally. She and Gregory Bateson had found themselves falling in love during that tour and so she and Reo Fortune were divorced. In 1935 Gregory Bateson came to the United States and their professional collaboration and personal relationship intensified. They were married in 1936, and they arrived in Bali in March of that year to do field work on a very personal, intensive level. They chose a village in which to live and built a house where they lived for two years. There they learned Balinese culture as it revealed itself through the lives of the natives of a simple village, recording the experience through Bateson's photographs and Margaret Mead's detailed notes. Since they lived in the village for two years, the team was able simultaneously to observe and experience Balinese life in all its dimensions. In that two year period Gregory Bateson took some twenty-five thousand photographs and Dr. Mead wrote volumes of notes based upon her own reactions to various examples of the Balinese culture including birth feasts, carved kitchen gods, paintings, village priests' prayers, villagers' clothing and villagers' everyday life and ceremonial habits and furniture. At the outbreak of World War II they returned home to work on a joint effort, *Balinese Character,* a fascinating account of their two year study of Balinese life. Margaret Mead discovered she could have a child after all, and shortly after the Batesons returned from Bali she gave birth to her only child, Catherine, on December 8, 1939.

Margaret Mead returned to Bali in 1956 with a colleague who photographed in new style some of the same things she had seen two decades earlier. She also returned to restudy the Manus in 1953, 1964, 1965, 1966, 1967, 1971 and 1975. There was, however, a new element in her life, in addition to the war, which precluded her doing any field work.

During the nearly two decade period that passed before Margaret Mead returned to the Admiralty Islands, World War II intervened and she devoted herself to motherhood, teaching, writing, and lecturing. Her career was as varied as ever, and she accepted a number of important positions in the world of letters and the social sciences. While she personally tended to her infant daughter, even breast feeding her, Dr. Mead taught at New York University. The following summer she commuted to Washington, D.C., where she worked at an assignment on cultural change. During that summer she also wrote *And Keep Your Powder*

Dry, a book which sought to establish the correlation between immigration and character formation in the United States. During the war she also served as Executive Secretary of the Committee on Food Habits of the National Research Council in Washington, D.C. as well as a lecturer in various American colleges and universities and in England as well. Those assignments in Washington were followed by studies of culture from which emerged several works in which she collaborated at a distance with others including *The Study of Culture at a Distance, Childhood in Contemporary Culture* and *Soviet Attitude towards Authority.*

By 1945 Margaret Mead and Gregory Bateson began to drift apart. Gregory ultimately remarried but she wrote subsequently: ". . . My years as a collaborating wife, trying to combine intensive field work and an intense personal life, also came to an end." She could no longer function or find fulfillment in simultaneously assuming both exacting roles.

Margaret Mead's exceptionally rich and varied career also included membership in the Department of Anthropology of the American Museum of Natural History in New York City and ultimately the position of Curator of Ethnology. As an academician she held several distinguished posts, most notably Adjunct Professor of Anthropology at Columbia University.

During the period after World War II Dr. Mead began working in a field that was of ever increasing interest and concern; namely, mental health. She became a member of the first research study group of the National Institute for Mental Health becoming president of the latter organization in 1956. As a visiting professor of anthropology in the department of psychiatry of the University of Cincinnati College of Medicine, she moved into this field on the academic level in 1957. In 1959 she became Sloan Professor at the Menninger School of Psychiatry.

Her fields of interest continued to expand in ensuing years into some of the most pressing social and political problems of the past several decades. In the field of race relations she showed her concern and interest by serving as trustee of Hampton Institute, the famous black college, from 1945, serving as co-editor of *Science and Race,* and co-author of *Rap on Race* with James Baldwin.

Concurrently, during these past several decades, she has served as a monthly columnist for *Redbook* magazine, has revisited the scenes of her field work in the '20's and '30's, for which she had learned six Pacific languages, has been the recipient of many awards and honorary degrees, such as the Viking Medal in General Anthropology, the Joseph Priestley Award, the Kalinga Prize for the Popularization of Science and the William Proctor Prize for Scientific Achievement, and served as member, officer and leader of a host of professional societies including President of the American Association for the Advancement of Science, President of the Scientists' Institute on Public Information and the Society for General Systems Research, and co-chairperson of the United States Task Force on the Future of Mankind and the Role of the Churches in a World of Science Based Technology. She helped to inaugurate a new department of anthropology at New York University and Fordham University's new Liberal Arts College at Lincoln Center in New York.

By the 1970's she also found herself in a personally satisfying role as a grandmother and mother-in-law. Catherine married Barkev Kassarjian and, as a young professional couple, they enjoy a rich, full life together. In 1970 Catherine gave birth to a daughter whom she named Sevann Margaret. The birth of the child was a particularly joyous event for the parents and for Margaret Mead since their first child, a boy named Martin was born prematurely in the Philippines, and lived only long enough to be christened and registered as a citizen. The young couple was scheduled to go on a two year teaching-research stint in Iran in 1972. Her daughter, granddaughter, and son-in-law provide an extra dimension to Dr. Mead's life.

Margaret Mead, in addition to being one of the world's most

distinguished anthropologists, and the author of twenty-seven books and hundreds of articles, has become one of the best known spokesmen of the intellectual community on a host of subjects of recent and common concern, among them the decriminalization of marijuana, black-white race relations, the generation gap, Women's Liberation and equal rights and opportunities for women, environmental pollution, population control, city planning and many others. Through her many appearances on popular radio and television talk shows, dozens of lectures throughout the country, numerous magazine articles and frequently appearing books, she has become not only highly visible and well known, but also an active and influential member of a host of commissions and committees. Her energy and her work continue to make her a popular figure with groups whose interests, ages, backgrounds, and cultures differ.

This is by no means a definitive treatment of all her achievements, positions and honors; however, they do reflect the prodigious energy and intellect which has made Margaret Mead one of the most creative thinkers of our time. More important though than the host of honors and prestigious positions that Margaret Mead has garnered throughout her adult life is the profound effect that she has had upon the thinking and the perceptions of the Western world. Her research disproved the commonly held notion that man is fundamentally competitive and that wars and poverty are inevitable consequences of that human trait. She showed, through her work with Pacific island groups, that societies exist where cooperation rather than competition and aggressiveness is the rule. Furthermore, she punctured the idea that men are innately aggressive and women essentially unaggressive by pointing to the three tribes she had studied in New Guinea where the reverse of the commonly accepted Western view of male and female behavior is the norm. Women, therefore, need not be limited to housework and motherhood.

Dr. Mead's insights into human nature emerged long before the Environmental Movement or Women's Liberation movements had achieved their present popularity. What they suggest, more than this brilliant anthropologist's advanced thinking, is her belief in the flexibility of the human personality and the potentialities of humankind. Cultures determine and develop human behavior and personality. If we can expand our understanding of men and women through this study of various cultures, we can look forward to possibly effecting a better world. It is that legacy of knowledge and hope that she has given to the world that has made Margaret Mead one of the towering intellects of the twentieth century.

A CURRENT BIBLIOGRAPHY

Margaret Mead is a prolific author. She has written dozens of books, pamphlets, articles and columns. She has not been the subject of a full-length work herself, so we have listed under writings about Margaret Mead, Dr. Mead's autobiography and several current articles of which she is the subject. In the main though, we have listed several books authored by Dr. Mead that you should read. The list is by no means comprehensive but it is appropriately selective.

Books About Margaret Mead

Mead, Margaret. *Blackberry Winter, My Earlier Years.* New York: William Morrow and Company, Inc., 1972.
Dempsey, David. "The Mead and Her Message," *The New York Times Magazine,* (April 26, 1970), 23.
———— "Provocative Prophetic Margaret Mead," *Readers' Digest,* (August, 1970), 127–131.
Sakal, J. "Remarkable Woman—Margaret Mead," *McCall's,* (June, 1970), 80–81.
———— "Margaret Mead Today: Mother to the World," *Time Magazine,* (March 21, 1969), 74.

Books by Margaret Mead

Blackberry Winter: My Earlier Years. New York: Morrow, 1972; reprinted in paperback, 1972, Touchstone Edition, New York: Simon and Schuster; 1975, New York: Pocket Books.

Coming of Age in Samoa. New York: Morrow, 1928; reprinted in paperback, 1961 (with new preface), Apollo Editions A-30, New York: Morrow.

Growing Up in New Guinea. New York: Morrow, 1930; reprinted 1975 (with new preface), New York: Morrow.

And Keep Your Powder Dry. New York: Morrow, 1942; reprinted 1965 (with new chapter), Apollo Editions A-105, New York: Morrow; 1971, Freeport, New York: Libraries Press.

New Lives for Old: Cultural Transformation—Manus, 1928–1953. New York: Morrow, 1956; reprinted 1975 (with new preface), New York: Morrow.

Culture and Commitment: A Study of the Generation Gap. Garden City, New York: Natural History Press/Doubleday, 1970; paperback edition, 1970.

A Rap on Race. Philadelphia and New York: Lippincott, 1971.

Male and Female. New York: Morrow, 1949; 1975, Paperback Editions, New York: Morrow.

Ruth Benedict. New York: Columbia University Press, 1974.

CHAPTER VIII

Marian Anderson

"Music and women I cannot but give way to, whatever my business is."

Samuel Pepys

A woman of extraordinary spiritual beauty, personal dignity and musical talent, Marian Anderson has won the hearts of men and women throughout the world during her more than half-century of public performances. Her life story began in a small house in urban Philadelphia and moved on to a personally designed "dream house" in the suburban splendors of Connecticut. Professionally, she has gone from church and public school choirs to the struggles of the college and club concert trails, and then on to spectacular tours of Europe, South America, Israel and the United States. Her career has spanned more than fifty years and been studded with countless spectacular triumphs. The moments that probably stand out most are her appearance at the Lincoln Memorial on Easter Sunday of 1939, her debut at the Metropolitan Opera on January 7, 1955 in Verdi's opera, *The Masked Ball,* and her two appearances at the White House. That a person who labored under the twofold handicap of being both a woman and a black was able to achieve so much personal and professional fulfillment is a tribute to the dedication of an extraordinary woman and artist, and to the American system

PHOTO BY COURTESY OF HUROK CONCERTS INC.

Marian Anderson

which afforded Marian Anderson the opportunities to achieve a rare measure of success.

Probably the most dramatic event in Miss Anderson's illustrious career centered about her scheduled appearance in Washington, D.C. in 1939 at Constitution Hall, an auditorium that was owned by the Daughters of the American Revolution, a staid and conservative organization. The day the newspapers carried the account of the refusal of the D.A.R. to allow Miss

Anderson to give a recital there, this dignified and talented artist was catapulted into the center of a social and political controversy. There was grim irony in the fact that the women of the D.A.R., who considered themselves the descendants of the very men and women who had fought to create a democratic country, were engaged in an act with blatantly racist overtones. Reaction was swift and widespread; a hue and cry arose throughout the country and abroad as well. Jascha Heifetz, the violin virtuoso, announced that he would cancel his scheduled appearance at Constitution Hall because, under the circumstances, he was ashamed to appear in the hall. Deems Taylor, the eminent musicologist, expressed the protests of the musical community of the nation. The most dramatic gesture was made by Mrs. Eleanor Roosevelt, the wife of President Roosevelt and the nation's First Lady, who announced publicly that she was resigning from the Daughters of the American Revolution. Capping the wave of protests was the formation of a people's committee which arranged for a public concert by Miss Anderson at the Lincoln Memorial on Easter Sunday of 1939.

Some seventy-five thousand people turned out for the concert to which Miss Anderson came escorted by a cadre of motorcycle police. The immense crowd included people of all religions, races, creeds and national origins. Among the most distinguished members of the audience were Secretary of the Interior Harold Ickes, Secretary of the Treasury Henry Morgenthau, United States Supreme Court Justice Hugo Black and many members of Congress. After a glowing introduction offered by Secretary Ickes, Marian Anderson stepped forward, serene and composed, to sing before a hushed audience. Her clear, rich voice rang out over the vast assemblage as she chose from her repertoire songs that had become favorites with her audiences through the years. "America," "Nobody Knows de Trouble I See," and other standards moved many rapt listeners to tears. Miss Anderson herself could barely contain her own emotions. It was more than a concert. It was an extraordinary emotional experience. Marian

Anderson had risen beyond her reputation as a great artist to become a kind of national symbol of the hopes and dreams of an oppressed minority, as well as the personification of one of the most famous steps for justice essayed by a nation ridden by the guilt of its years of racism.

Marian Anderson bloomed in a family that was immersed in the world of music and song. Her parents were natives of Virginia and lived their early years in an atmosphere replete with the stirring sounds of spirituals and work songs and the gay rhythms of banjo and guitar music. Their love of music carried over into their everyday lives even when they moved from the rural South to the urban sprawl of Philadelphia.

Marian Anderson was born in a small house in South Philadelphia in 1902. For many years, even after she had received international acclaim, this outstanding coloratura soprano made her permanent home with her mother in a comfortable house on the very same block to which her parents had come several decades before.

Mrs. Anderson had been a teacher in Virginia, and she could have taught in Philadelphia; however, she decided to devote almost all of her energies to taking care of her family. Throughout her life she maintained the bearing of a well educated cultured woman. Mr. Anderson was a hardworking man and a highly respected member of the community. He served as an usher in the Union Baptist Church and ran a small coal and ice delivery business while adding to his meager income through a variety of odd jobs that were available around the city. Mrs. Anderson also tried to supplement the family income by performing a variety of difficult low-paying jobs such as house servant, caretaker, or washerwoman. Marian eventually began to help in raising her two younger sisters, as the eldest child in the family, when both her parents were forced to work because of economic difficulties. It was in this closely knit family world of love, music, hard work and religion that the character of Marian Anderson was molded. These were childhood impressions that were to leave an indelible imprint upon her throughout her life.

Despite the difficulties they faced during those years, the family enjoyed many heartwarming and rich experiences. Among them were a big outing each year to the Barnum and Bailey Circus, holiday celebrations and shopping sprees at Easter time and sharing in their father's church work. The warmth of a family that enjoyed each other's company and savored commonly shared experiences takes on particular meaning in a modern world where families are becoming increasingly fragmented and polarized.

Before she was even six years of age Marian was an active participant in the life of the church. She attended Sunday school and the religious services, and shortly after her sixth birthday she was enrolled in the church's junior choir. Here her love for music, already cultivated by her aunt and father who loved to sing and who always urged the girls to sing and to play a musical instrument, blossomed in the warmth of the church.

At the age of six she developed a keen desire to own a violin. Having earned some of her own money scrubbing the steps of neighbors' houses, Marian set her sights on purchasing a violin from a local pawnshop. The cost of the violin was $3.98, by today's standards a modest sum, but the young girl scrubbed countless steps and ran innumerable errands to earn the money for its purchase. When she finally was able to bring the violin home she was ecstatic. Her violin was a triumph of persistence and love of music. By the time Marian was eight the Anderson family had added a piano to its musical equipment.

Coupled with her work on the musical instruments was the talented girl's singing work with the church's junior choir. Mr. Alexander Robinson, who led the junior choir, was not a trained teacher of music; however, he transmitted to his charges his natural skill and deep love of music. He also encouraged Marian's early public singing appearances in various local churches, clubs and societies. She was gaining invaluable experience through this medium and at a relatively tender age she had engaged in a substantial number of public appearances. She developed a local reputation and soon began singing in school concerts as well. Friends and admirers in her church raised small sums of money to allow her the opportunity to receive formal training in music from professional teachers. Marian was actually only eight when she was being publicized as a ten year old contralto, a reflection of her budding talent when she was still so very young.

Her tenth year remained imprinted upon her memory for another reason though. It was during that year that her father died after an accidental blow to the head. The bereaved family then moved in with their grandparents. Tragedy had struck the Anderson family and the course of their lives was irrevocably changed thereafter. Grandmother was a hardworking loving woman who had "scads of children" living with her all the time. Grandfather was a Black Jew, a quiet man, dominated by his wife. He observed Saturday as his Sabbath, attended services at the Temple and celebrated holidays such as Passover. Their aunt ran the household and Mother worked by the day and occasionally took in laundry. There was an atmosphere of life and vitality generated by the noisy shouts of children, the required chores given everyone in the busy household and the backbreaking labors engaged in by the uncomplaining women in the household including the grandmother, mother, and aunt. Yet there was family unity, music, religion, and a home to give everyone a sense of security.

Marian Anderson started her secondary school career at William Penn High School where she was enrolled in a commercial course which she soon discovered was not to her liking. It was only in the weekly music period that she found satisfaction. The music teacher quickly provided her with opportunities to sing in the school chorus and on occasion to do small solos. Once, after she had sung a solo at an assembly program, she was summoned to the principal's office where she heard a visitor urge the principal to see to it that the fledgling singer was transferred from the commercial course to a straight academic, college preparatory course so that she could be given as much music training as possible.

When Marian transferred to South Philadelphia High School, a more progressive school, she met Dr. Lucy Wilson, who was not only the principal but also a great teacher and source of inspiration to thousands of girls. She took a personal interest in her young charge, the first white person to do so. She was a creative educator who arranged interesting assemblies to which prominent persons were invited to perform or to speak. Students would also perform at these assemblies. It was after one of these assemblies at which Marian sang that she met Lia Roma, a friend of Dr. Wilson's, who was subsequently quite helpful to her.

Music and the church began to envelop Marian's life completely. She made public appearances with increasing frequency. The church's choir began to attract an ever widening audience and she soon caught the eye and ear of Roland Hayes, a distinguished tenor who became her inspiration. He recommended that she receive professional training and suggested the name of a teacher. The church congregation, led by its pastor, took up a collection to help the aspiring young singer.

Soon Marian Anderson was appearing as a soloist before various church, social and fraternal groups, singing as often as three times in one night. Payments varied from a "thank you" to a minimum five dollar fee. On at least one occasion the chairlady of a committee asked the teenager to perform for an impending function and was stunned by the insistence upon a $5 fee to which she finally agreed. Her local fame was enhanced by her joining the Philadelphia Choral Society, composed of outstanding members of the various black church choirs in Philadelphia, where she sang for the sheer joy of the experience. One of the members of that group predicted, in a conversation with Mrs. Anderson, that someday Marian would earn as much as $50 an appearance! With the help of Ronald

Hayes, it was a prediction that was to prove to be an understatement.

Her solo appearances began to multiply, and she was soon accepting engagements out of town, in the areas surrounding Philadelphia. These short tours to Negro colleges and churches gave her the additional experience and exposure that she needed at this particular time. It was around this period of her life that Marian became aware of the need for more sound singing training. Through a family acquaintance she was introduced to a distinguished woman named Samdess Patterson, a brilliant soprano and singing teacher. When Mrs. Patterson learned that Marian was unable to pay the $1 per session fee that she charged, she volunteered to teach the girl free of charge because of her dedication to the development of fine young singers. During the few months that she served as Marian's teacher, this devoted woman taught her how to use her voice, familiarized her with her first Schumann songs, arranged class concerts and even presented the girl with her first evening gown.

While striving to further her musical education Marian Anderson first encountered blatant racism. When she went to enroll at a music school in Philadelphia she was told in cold and abrupt fashion, "We don't take colored." This first cruel confrontation with race prejudice was a shock to Marian, but it was unfortunately not the last experience of this sort. On a railroad trip to her first gala concert in Savannah, Georgia, while accompanied by her mother, Marian found her bags moved to the first car, the Jim Crow car for blacks only, when the train reached Washington, D.C. This experience with railroad segregation was duplicated shortly thereafter when on tour she and her accompanist, Billy King, were able to eat in the dining car only because they were served in the curtained off section used by the waiters as their dining area. Segregated waiting rooms and other facilities, faulty reservation arrangements, and frequently inferior housing accommodations were among the many humiliations to which this sensitive black singing artist was subjected to during those early years of her career. They were indignities that she never forgot and to which would be added many more during the ensuing years, but instead of antagonizing or embittering her, they served to further strengthen her character and resolve.

Marian Anderson's pursuit of formal musical training was part of that resolve. When it became clear that Mrs. Patterson had given her talented student the foundation that she needed, she urged that a new teacher be engaged and soon the black contralto was working with Agnes Reinsnyder, a leading white contralto and singing teacher in Philadelphia. She gave the high school senior help in developing her medium and low tones and in improving her breath control. Shortly before she was graduated from high school Marian was introduced to Guiseppe Boghetti, who remained her teacher until his death. It was through Lia Roma, her high school principal's friend, that Mr. Boghetti and Miss Anderson established a fruitful pupil-teacher relationship that was to stand her in good stead throughout her career. Once again though, the problem of paying for her lessons arose, but this time the Union Baptist Church organized a concert among whose soloists was Roland Hayes. The $600 realized from that event was used to engage Mr. Boghetti as her teacher.

He was an exacting teacher. She was gradually transformed into a highly disciplined, expressive professional singer. Mr. Boghetti gave her musical training, worked on her programs with her and served not only as an effective teacher, but also as a highly valued counselor and critic. During her years with him Miss Anderson's tours increased, but she always returned for training and advice as often as her schedule would allow.

It was during this period that it became apparent that Miss Anderson needed a manager to help her. Billy King soon doubled in brass as her accompanist and manager. Her personal and professional life was taking on a more complex quality and so she recognized the need for this kind of support. A Town Hall concert in New York, the purchase of a new home for her family, her first recording of "Heaven, Heaven" and "Deep River," and an ever increasing tempo of concert tours made her life that much more full and harried at the same time.

The person who provided particular balance during this time of struggle and uncertainty was Mrs. Anderson. A woman who worked hard all her life, who retained a lifelong deep religious faith and fierce loyalty to her family, she was molded in the traditional cast of the totally loving and supportive mother.

Guiseppe Boghetti arranged for the particular event which led to Marian Anderson's achieving a major step towards national prominence. He entered her in a Lewisohn Stadium concert contest in which some three hundred contestants from throughout the country competed. Miss Anderson won the contest and the prize to appear as a soloist at Lewisohn Stadium on the night of August 26, 1925 with the internationally famous New York Philharmonic Orchestra before a jam packed audience. She received favorable reviews from the critics and soon found that her concert engagements and fees were increased accordingly. Invitations for appearances poured in from all over the United States and Canada. Stardom appeared to be imminent. The road to that height was still to be strewn with disappointments and frustration.

Some time after her appearance at Lewisohn Stadium Miss Anderson appeared at Carnegie Hall as soloist with the Hall Johnson choir. Soon she was under the management of Arthur Judson, one of the most outstanding concert managers in the country. Her fees rose from $300 to $500 per performance, though during that first year under the Arthur Judson banner Miss Anderson had fewer engagements. Still, she felt that her career was at a standstill and made up her mind that a European stay would be helpful. Against the advice of her manager Miss Anderson decided to embark for Europe.

It was by no means an easy decision for Miss Anderson to make since finances were limited and she hesitated at abandoning her American concert career and leaving her family. But encouraged by her family, her friends and Billy King, she embarked for Europe in the late summer of 1930. Once there, she stayed in England, functioning primarily as a student rather than as a concert artist. She had not earned very much money in Europe and so when her funds began to run out, Miss Anderson returned home.

Upon her return home Miss Anderson discovered that her concert career had slowed down and before long she decided that she had to return to Europe. She felt that she must work on lieder (songs) in German and had to go to Germany to study. With the help of a Julius Rosenwald Fund fellowship she was able to do so. There she studied German lieder and began preparations for a full-length Berlin concert which she gave in October, 1930. Before the concert she met, in the studio of her lieder teacher, Kosti Venahen, a Finnish pianist who was to serve as her accompanist for ten years on many of her European and South American tours. Her Berlin concert was well received by both audience and critics. That Berlin appearance though, was to be her last one in Germany until 1950 when she sang under the auspices of the Allied occupation forces.

While appearing in Scandinavia, during the years Adolph Hitler was in power, she was asked whether she was available to sing in Germany and whether she was Aryan, pure-bred German. Miss Anderson was not, of course, and once again she suffered from race prejudice, this time in Europe. Soon after she was booked on a successful Scandinavian tour which was to be one of the major stepping stones in her rise to international prominence as a major concert artist.

With Kosti Venahen serving as her accompanist, the young black concert artist slowly and surely sang her way into the hearts of the blond and fair Norwegians, Danes and Finns. For many of the members of her audience this was their first sight of a Negro. During her concert tour she also studied Scandinavian music, had a memorable hour with Jan Sibelius, the great Finnish composer, and enjoyed the privilege of meeting the President of Finland. One of the most memorable experiences on this tour was a benefit concert in a Danish prison for hardened life term prisoners. It was a moving experience for her as well as for those men who were being exposed to a rare bit of beauty in their desperate and dreary lives.

The Scandinavian tour, which ran from September, 1933 to April, 1934 and involved Miss Anderson in an exhausting schedule of 142 concerts, soon led to demands for her appearance in countries throughout Europe. From May, 1934 to December, 1935 she appeared in many other European countries including Switzerland, Holland, Belgium, Poland, Austria, France, England and Russia. Her Russian tour was a successful and fascinating one as Miss Anderson moved across the vast stretches of the U.S.S.R., visiting dozens of cities and provinces, struck by the people's genuine hunger for music, and, on occasion, getting a disturbing hint of the totalitarian aspects of the society, particularly when her accompanist took photographs, which was prohibited in the U.S.S.R., and when they gave money to a woman secretly begging, another activity strictly forbidden in Russia.

These resounding professional successes were duplicated in many other European countries, but it was Miss Anderson's 1934 concert in Paris that crystallized her fame and made her name synonymous with superb singing artistry throughout the world. Singing classical opera arias, Russian and Scandinavian folk songs, and Negro spirituals, she established herself as a superb soprano of great versatility and one with an impressive repertoire. It was in Paris that she met Sol Hurok, one of the greatest concert managers and impressarios of all time, who was to become her manager, propelling her to superstardom, and remaining in that capacity until his death in 1974.

The European tour was a celebration as much as it was a concert tour. In each country or city at least one experience made the event a particularly memorable one. Having sung in Berlin and Salzburg, she also performed before King Gustav in Stockholm and King Christian in Copenhagen. In Rome, after singing before the Crown Princess and various lords and ladies, she began to move out of the room. A horrified protocol officer rushed to her side to advise her that queens always left first!

In Salzburg Miss Anderson had a unique experience. Appearing before some of the greatest names in the world of music, at that time including famed singer Lotte Lehman and the immortal symphony orchestra conducters Arturo Toscanini and Bruno Walter, as well as a cardinal of the church and other religious personages, she sang a short program including a few Schubert songs, a song by Brahms and several Negro spirituals including one of her best, "Crucifixion." After she sang "Crucifixion" the distinguished audience paid her a rare tribute. There was absolute silence as everyone sat transfixed. No sound or applause could be appropriate to the moment. Following the concert Toscanini described Miss Anderson's voice as one that persons were privileged to hear but once every hundred years. Coming from one of the supreme masters of music this was high praise indeed. Other such experiences greeted her in Spain, Senegal, Dakar, Rio de Janeiro, Buenos Aires, Montevideo and other areas of the world.

Her dramatic return to the United States was eased by her highly acclaimed European tour. A great homecoming concert was arranged in New York for December 30, 1935. This dramatic occasion was to be made even more memorable by an exceptional example of personal courage by Miss Anderson. Returning by boat from Europe, she broke her ankle just before the boat docked and only one day before the concert. Unwilling to disappoint her many American admirers she decided to go on despite the urgent pleas of her doctors and friends. Spurning the use of a wheel chair, she appeared on stage in a gown long enough to conceal the cast on her broken foot. She stood throughout the concert and gave her full program despite the excruciating pain that she suffered every moment she stood on the stage. Her audience, of course, was stunned and then wildly enthusiastic when they learned of the reason for her stiff bows and her leaning on the piano. That first concert was the beginning of Miss Anderson's tremendous reception throughout the United States. These tours and triumphs both here and abroad were to be repeated many times throughout the coming years as she regaled her audiences with her repertoire of some two hundred songs sung in nine languages.

On two separate occasions Marian Anderson has appeared at the White House. The first time she sang at a small party in the President's private apartment. Mrs. Anderson, Marian's mother, was invited for the occasion and she was deeply affected by the honor of being invited to meet President Roosevelt. The second time Queen Elizabeth and King George were on an official tour in this country and, when they were guests of President and Mrs. Roosevelt, the first couple of the land chose Marian Anderson to be among the great artists to entertain the Royal Family. As a token of their gratitude President and Mrs. Roosevelt sent Miss Anderson a framed and autographed picture of themselves.

The scope of Marian Anderson's tours has been literally world-wide, going from North to South and East to West. In Japan she appeared in the palace before the Empress after a special entertainment had been staged for her. Following her performance Miss Anderson was given several gifts by the Empress.

Israel was a travel-tour experience that had a particular impact upon this member of an oppressed people. She felt the spirit of the long suffering Jewish people, many of whom were refugees from the concentration and death camps of Europe and Adolph Hitler. The efforts of this young nation to forge a new destiny for its people had a profound effect upon Marian Anderson. Each performance in a refugee camp, a kibbutz (collective colony), or a concert hall was a moment to treasure as she responded to her audiences' tremendous thirst for music and beauty. As a Christian, she felt a particular religious experience as she did the Stations of the Cross in Jerusalem, crossed the Jordan River and visited the Mount of Olives and the Dead Sea.

As one of the world's greatest interpreters of Negro spirituals these moments took on special meaning for her.

January 7, 1955 represented another jewel in Marian Anderson's professional crown for, on that evening, she was given the one final element of recognition that had been heretofore denied her. At a party given by her manager, Sol Hurok, she met Rudolf Bing, general manager of the Metropolitan Opera Company, who came right up to her and in direct fashion asked her if she would be interested in singing at the Met. Stunned and almost incredulous (after all, the Metropolitan is the greatest opera house in the world), Miss Anderson agreed. She was offered the role of Ulrica, the old sorceress in Verdi's *The Masked Ball*. In characteristic fashion, Marian Anderson began intensive work in preparation for the role. Though a long established star, she felt it necessary to study hard because opera was a new medium for her, and because she had both a particular personal and professional stake in this part. The performance on January 7, 1955 represented another memorable evening for this great singer. When the curtain rose on the second scene, which marked Miss Anderson's performance, the applause rose to a crescendo before she had even sung a single note. Needless to say her performance was greeted with respect and with enthusiasm. The following week she experienced a particular thrill when she repeated her performance in her home town, Philadelphia. By her own admission this was a highlight of her life. It meant so much to Miss Anderson and to her people for she was the first black to sing as a regular member of the company of the august opera house. She felt that she was opening the doors for great black singing artists such as Mattwilda Dobbs, Leontyne Price, Lawrence Winters and others.

Much well deserved praise and success has been Miss Anderson's lot; however, in addition to the many flattering comments and critiques that have been showered upon her, she has all too often been subjected to the cruelties of racial prejudice. At times she was denied proper train, hotel or dining accommodations because of her color, regardless of being a world renowned artist. On one occasion, Miss Anderson aroused a furor among some people because she had come out in response to an ovation holding the hand of her accompanist, Franz Rupp, with whom she took a bow. There were those who took exception to the sight of a black and a white holding hands. On another occasion, while in the white waiting room of a Southern town railroad station with her white hosts, she was summarily and hastily asked to leave. Her white hosts left in protest with her. To these various slights Miss Anderson responded with her customary dignity and poise. She refused to sing before segregated audiences, but this was the extent of her protest against a deplorable, cruel, and inhumane practice.

Marian Anderson has become in her lifetime a legend as an artist and as a person. Her rich, expressive voice is considered one of the most exquisite of our time, and she has been ranked as one of the great concert artists of the world. Beyond that, she has come to exemplify the longings of an oppressed minority group for freedom and fulfillment in the face of centuries of repression. Of this first lady of the concert stage it can truly be said that "She (He) Has the Whole World in Her (His) Hands" by virtue of her artistic power and personal magnetism. Underlying this is a way of life and a personal philosophy that can best be summarized by the closing lines of her autobiography, *My Lord, What a Morning,* when she says: "Not everyone can be turned aside from meaness and hatred, but the great majority of Americans is heading in that direction. I have a great belief in the future of my people and my country." Those are words and ideas that should be a call to thought and action for all of us.

A CURRENT BIBLIOGRAPHY

Anderson, Marian. *My Lord, What a Morning.* New York: The Viking Press, 1956.
Newman, Shirlee P. *Marian Anderson: Lady from Philadelphia.* New York: Westminster Press, 1966.

Tobias, Tobi. *Marian Anderson.* (A Crowell Biography). New York: Thomas Y. Crowell, 1972.

Venahen, Kosti. *Marian Anderson: A Portrait.* New York: McGraw-Hill Book Co., Inc., 1941.

CHAPTER IX

Gloria Steinem

"A witty woman is a treasure"
George Meredith

The twentieth century has witnessed some of the most dramatic and far reaching political, technological, and social movements in world history. The development of variations of Communism in the Soviet Union and in China, the revolution of rising expectations, the Black Power movement, anti-colonialism in Africa and Asia, the "new morality," automation, the youth revolution and the atomic age are among the most far-reaching and momentous of these movements. One of the most interesting of all these phenomena has been the burgeoning Women's Liberation movement. At first dismissed by "male chauvinist" pigs and even by most women as a passing fad, it has become a formidable force for change in the status of women in the United States. Several recent court decisions have borne out this radical change. As a result of class actions which asserted that sexual prejudice had led to their being discriminated against professionally, women at Rutgers University, the International Telephone and Telegraph Company and the Bank of America have won sizable financial settlements and highly significant court decisions that suggest that sexual discrimination is real and will be treated accordingly by the courts. Probably the most articu-

PHOTO BY ANN PHILLIPS

Gloria Steinem

late, effective, and highly visible spokesperson for the feminist movement in the United States is Gloria Steinem. As a journalist, publicist, social critic, magazine editor and television personality, she has been this country's leading standard bearer for the Women's Liberation movement. She became an adherent and proponent of feminism at the height of her career as a "pop" culture personality, one of the most sought after women because of her physical beauty, keen intelligence, and capacity for communication.

Gloria Steinem was born in Toledo, Ohio on March 25, 1934. (There are several publications that list other, earlier dates of birth.) She was the younger daughter of Ruth and Leo Steinem and the product of a religiously mixed marriage. Her father was Jewish and her mother French Protestant. Her family background is interesting in light of her present claim to fame. As the granddaughter of Mrs. Pauline Steinem, one of this country's early feminist leaders who served as president of the Ohio Women's Suffrage Association and was also one of the two United States delegates to the 1908 meeting of the International Council of Women, Gloria was in a sense almost weaned on belief in the equality of the sexes.

Leo Steinem was a dreamer. An antique dealer and summer resort operator, his family followed him around the country while living in a trailer. It was a twofold source of pride to him that he had never worn a hat or held down a job. He was always planning to make a movie, cut a record, create a new beverage, or build a new hotel. Before she had reached her teenage years, Gloria's parents were divorced, and she and Ruth Steinem moved back to East Toledo where the mother resumed newspaper reporting, a career she had abandoned when she assumed the roles of wife and mother.

Gloria's life took on a more stable character during this Toledo period. She attended school regularly for the first time and took tap dancing lessons. She even won a local television station talent contest. Nonetheless, the impressionable and spirited young girl found life in Toledo quite depressing. She lived in a slum area of East Toledo in a rat infested neighborhood where you did not sleep with your toes exposed unless you wanted to have them bitten off by the preying rodents. Salvation came for Gloria in her senior year in high school when she went to live in Washington with her older sister. Washington, D.C. was a revelation to Gloria. Life was more leisurely, and she met boys who read books and were culturally oriented.

Her high school grades were low, but on the strength of outstanding scores on the College Board examination, she was admitted to Smith College, one of the nation's most prestigious women's colleges. After her high school graduation in Washington in 1952, Gloria's mother financed her four years at Smith with money she had garnered from the sale of their house in Toledo. Gloria seemed to blossom in college where she became an outstanding student. Various honors came her way, among them scholarships, election to Phi Beta Kappa and being graduated magna cum laude.

Gloria Steinem was graduated from Smith College in 1956 as a government major. After graduation she left for India on a two year fellowship where she studied at the universities in Calcutta and New Delhi. Her two year stay in India inspired her with an impelling need to apprise the people of this country of what was going on in Asia and the obvious necessity of getting the American people to recognize the consequences of economic and political instability in Asia. She became painfully aware of the horrors of malnutrition, starvation and overpopulation as well as the impact of racism on a society. Her experiences in India were to have considerable effect upon the liberal leanings that she posited in later years when she espoused the causes of blacks, Hispanics, migrant farm workers, women and other oppressed groups. Gloria Steinem subsequently became a leading advocate of liberal causes and a highly visible activist because of those experiences.

She sought a position as a reporter, a logical avenue for her to channel her missionary zeal, but was unable to find a job. Instead, she accepted a position as the director of the Independent Research Service in Cambridge, Massachusetts, an organization which encouraged American students to go to Communist Youth Festivals in Vienna in 1959 and in Helsinki in 1962.

While she found certain satisfactions in her job, Gloria Steinem was anxious to come to New York, the hub of intellectual and literary life in the United States. In 1960 she arrived with the express purpose of making it as a writer. Her initial efforts were by no means crowned with particular success. She wrote several unsigned pieces for *Esquire* magazine before she earned her first by-line in the 1962 college issue with an article about the sexual revolution on the college campuses of the nation. That article, entitled "The Moral Disarmament of Betty Coed," with its keen insights on the dilemma of women in our country unprepared to cope with newly found freedom and the "new morality" and the birth control pill, was a professional watershed for Gloria Steinem.

On the strength of that article she got her first big assignment, an exposé of Playboy Club operations. Assuming the role of a Playboy Club Bunny at the New York Playboy Club, Ms. Steinem got an inside look at its operations during the month-long period that she played the role of Bunny. She wrote of that male chauvinist's dream house a highly amusing, pointed, two-part exposé which led to many new writing assignments.

Her writing assignments now came from some of the most famous and best paying magazines in America. Gloria Steinem began writing for magazines such as *McCalls, Cosmopolitan, Ladies Home Journal, Vogue, Life* and *Look*. She wrote on a variety of subjects, gaining new breadth by her experiences as a television script writer for the NBC-TV comedy show *That Was the Week That Was*. The television writing assignment during the 1964–1965 season honed her ability to write quickly topical subjects under the pressure of deadlines.

She also branched out into another writing field in the 1960's when she collaborated on a book on sun worshippers with a designer and illustrator. *The Beach Book* was essentially a picture book and not a very serious piece of work, but it was noteworthy for having a preface written by John Kenneth Galbraith, the distinguished Harvard professor, author, and diplomat, who was a long time friend and admirer of Ms. Steinem. He had declared that she was one of the three most important women he had ever met, high praise from a man who was on friendly terms with some of the most famous and powerful women in the world including Mrs. Jacqueline Kennedy Onassis.

Throughout the early and middle years of the 1960's Gloria Steinem was in great demand as a writer. Her work, however, was limited to the light, almost frivolous pieces that women's magazines thrived upon—articles about movie stars, pop culture, current fads and singing stars. Her proposals for more serious political articles were rejected since those topics were supposedly inappropriate for women journalists. She also became a celebrity of sorts in her own right, often being seen in the company of famous men such as Mike Nichols, the movie director, and Ted Sorenson, former aide to President Kennedy. She had "arrived," having achieved some measure of fame as a journalist and as a "pop" culture personality.

In 1968 she also helped to found *New York,* a weekly magazine. Its editor, Clay Felker, engaged Gloria Steinem as a contributing editor. What made the assignment particularly significant was the fact that she was given an opportunity to write about the American political, social, and economic scene. This opportunity represented a virtual 180 degree turn from the frivolous to the more serious vein of writing. Her articles on homosexuality, the political scene, the disintegration of conventional marriages, and the birth control pill gained her a new and particularly attentive audience. Those articles, coupled with a column entitled "The City Politic" in which she expressed her personal opinions of various political candidates and causes, gave her a new platform and additional exposure. Before long she moved along the inevitable road towards actual endorsement of a political candidate.

The 1968 Presidential campaign was enlivened by the candidacy of Senator Eugene McCarthy of Minnesota. Early in the pre-convention maneuvering Gloria Steinem endorsed Senator

McCarthy, about whom there had developed a mystique among the high school and college students and the intellectual community. She soon became disenchanted with him though and gave her support to Robert Kennedy. At the Democratic convention, Gloria Steinem roamed through the convention hall and sat in the hotel rooms where the behind-the-scenes business of the convention took place. She also found grist for her columnist's mill as an observer of the Republican Campaign Caravan in September, 1968. One of her columns during that period gave a rather critical evaluation of Richard Nixon and that treatment resulted in an extraordinary interview with Mrs. Patricia Nixon during which Mrs. Nixon lost her temper and had rather harsh words for "all those people who had it so easy." It was a rare outburst for the wife of the man who was to become President of the United States in 1968 and Gloria Steinem and her journalistic star reached new heights.

Gloria Steinem's political posture tends to incline to the left. She opposed the war in Indochina, generally supported the liberal wing of the Democratic party, and she is an inveterate supporter of causes such as reproductive freedom, ecology, migrant farm workers and minority group members ranging from blacks and Hispanics to Indians and Eskimos. She was an ardent supporter in 1969 of novelist Norman Mailer's bid for the mayor's office in New York and the Presidential drive of Senator George McGovern.

It was Gloria Steinem's involvement in the Women's Liberation movement that propelled her onto stage center of the national political and social scene. Her participation in the feminist drive towards equal rights and opportunities came about as the result of attending a meeting in November, 1969 of the Redstockings, a New York City Women's Liberation organization. Gloria Steinem went in her capacity as a columnist for *New York* magazine and, while she wrote a prize winning article on the budding Women's Liberation movement, she became a convert to the cause. As a result of that meeting she came to recognize that the barriers and problems that she had faced were part of an all pervasive political situation rather than merely personal inconveniencies that she had suffered. From that initial meeting there evolved Ms. Steinem's philosophy that man perpetuated the exploitation of women for economic, political and social reasons, consciously or subconsciously.

Gloria Steinem had found the primary *raison d'etre* for her personal and professional life. She became one of the Women's Liberation Movement's most active, articulate, and aggressive propagandists through her many personal appearances on the lecture circuit, her exposure on nation wide television programs, and, of course, through her role as a working journalist. Wearing any number of hats within the movement, she became one of its most effective speakers, fund raisers, organizers and publicists.

In 1970 she joined forces with Betty Friedan, author of *The Feminine Mystique,* and one of the movement's most powerful figures, and several other women to plan the strategy for the August 1970 Women's Strike for Equality, the feminists' first effort on the national scene. She worked with Congresswomen Bella Abzug and Shirley Chisholm in 1971 to found the National Women's Political Caucus. Gloria Steinem had seen fit to help found that group because she knew that the repression of women would be lessened by work on the political level. The organization, therefore, was formed to encourage women to run for political office and to endorse any and all political candidates who supported the women's rights effort. This mobilization of women's political power was followed by the formation of the Women's Action Alliance, a broadbased and nonpolitical organization that took as its primary aim the effort to free women of the shackles of their sex.

In 1971 Gloria Steinem began exploring the possibility of founding a new consumer magazine for women, one with an emphasis on encouraging and helping women to gain control over their lives. That magazine, entitled *Ms.,* received considerable support from various segments of society, and started regular monthly publication in July 1972. Patricia Carbine, former editor of McCall's magazine has been publisher since July, 1972. It represented the first major magazine in this country to be owned and operated by women. It focuses primarily on the changing role of women in American society and refuses all ads that it considers insulting to women. The titles of some of the articles that have appeared in the magazine in the last two years are indicative of its particular slant. "Is Romance Dead?," "Is It Kosher to Be Feminist?," "Down With Sexist Upbringing," and "Can Women Love Women?" reflect the new morality and the new image of women that is the linchpin of the magazine's thematic underpinning. In the first issue of the publication a list was provided of more than fifty women who are prominent in public life who admitted to having had one or more abortions, among them Gloria Steinem.

This independent cast of mind is also evident in Ms. (as she prefers to be called) Steinem's personal life. An attractive and handsomely endowed woman, she makes no conscious effort to be a sex symbol; however, she does not hide her light under a bushel either. She dresses in mod fashion, affects stylish glasses, and wears her brown-blond streaked hair long, with a part down the middle. An appealing woman both physically and intellectually, she continues to be escorted by highly eligible and successful men. She does not, however, believe in conventional marriage and has expressed deep reservations about motherhood. She admits to having had a number of "little marriages," but has remained free of any long or permanent arrangements. McCalls Magazine named her Woman of the Year in 1972 and one can understand why she was chosen.

Along with Betty Friedan, Congresswoman Bella Abzug and Congresswoman Shirley Chisholm, she represents the highest level of leadership in the Women's Liberation movement. She is the movement's most sought after spokesperson, its most effective fund-raiser, its most publicized personality, and its most valued public relations expert. She is often suspect because of her glamour and her apparent success as a mere sex object. But, in fact, she is respected as a journalist, speaker and thinker, particularly in the area of the feminist movement. Even her detractors admit that she manages to embody both form and substance with extraordinary results.

Despite all this chic and accomplishment, Gloria Steinem is quite selfless in many respects. She lectures in the company of other women's liberationists, preferably a black, and she passes writing assignments to fellow female journalists. Her generosity is particularly evident when one considers that she accepts women of all persuasion—radicals, lesbians, Democrats, and revolutionaries. She serves as counsellor-confidante to many women, treating them all with unfailing courtesy and sympathy.

Gloria Steinem's perception of the status of women in this country is one of political exploitation. In her judgment, one that is by no means original or unique, the political system dominated as it has been by men heretofore, is geared to the control and subjugation of women. It was consistent with her thinking that in the early 1970's she wrote an article for a national magazine on why the country needs a woman President. Her strong political views took particular form in the late 1960's and early 1970's when she withheld forty per cent of her tax payment which she said would go to support the war in Vietnam to which she was strenuously opposed. She continues to express her views in both aggressive and articulate fashion through the media of the magazines and talk show television programs. Her position is not always a popular one, but no one can deny that she and her colleagues have had an impact on the image and role of women in this country. In 1969 the Gallup Poll reported that fifty-four per cent of the people polled said they would vote for a qualified woman for President. By the summer of 1971 some sixty-six per cent of those polled said they would support a woman's quest for the Presidency.

Ms. Steinem has very strong feelings on a variety of matters related to the status and role of women in our culture. She is not in favor of marriage in its conventional form. According to her, marriage makes an individual legally half a person and who would want to marry half a person. While Ms. Steinem believes that it is possible for two people to live together in a loving, equal partnership, the legal institution of marriage works against that. Married people are one person and that person is the man. When a woman marries she loses her civil rights becoming a kind of "legal child" once more. While there can be loving partnerships, the institution of marriage works against it. As for having children, Ms. Steinem is uncertain. She sees certain pleasures and fulfillment in that role for women, but she also sees women who become mothers as virtual slaves.

This concept of women as bondswomen she says is particularly evident among housewives. Ms. Steinem sees housewives as members of one of society's most exploited groups since they work as much as one hundred hours a week on the average without pay or genuine appreciation. She says that men and children should share a housewife's chores, that she should be given a salary, and that she should be allowed freedom of choice to pursue another career.

She takes a dim view of women who play a passive role, a posture that has been assigned to them throughout history. Again she says that women should have freedom of choice to be aggressive or passive in sex, business, the arts, the professions, their homes or in any other activity. Gloria Steinem rejects the stereotype of women as the "weaker sex" and contends that this is a role that is not natural to women but rather one that has been foisted upon them by male chauvinists throughout the ages.

Her open minded view extends even in the area of human sexuality. She accepts all forms of that activity ranging from heterosexual to homosexual practices, and she has raised her voice on behalf of freedom of choice in this area as well. She is in favor of women's right to have an abortion. Despite bitter and often personal comments directed towards her because of her views, Ms. Steinem has remained steadfast and unfazed by the barrage of criticism.

When confronted by the assertion that many women are quite content in their roles as wives and mothers Ms. Steinem makes an interesting point. She says those who feel this way are entitled to feel and say so and to live their lives accordingly. What she hopes for though is that women are saying and doing so by choice and not because they have been brain washed. As she says about so many of the issues that revolve around women and their lives, "The point is choice—freedom of choice."

The answer for women, according to its most eloquent and best known spokeswoman, is political action through the Women's Liberation Movement and organizations such as NOW (The National Organization of Women) and the NWPC (the National Women's Political Caucus). Women must unite to elect those public officials, particularly women, who will fight for the equality of women and all oppressed minorities, for the cause of enduring peace and for the reformation of tax and marriage and abortions laws and child care legislation. These organizations are devoted to helping those political candidates who are dedicated to opposing sexism, violence, racism and poverty.

The thought of having a woman as President of the U.S. somehow seems remote to many of us. The old adage that "If you wish it, it need not be a dream," takes on particular meaning in the context of Ms. Steinem's impressive life story and the significant strides that the women's rights movement has made in a relatively short time. Ms. Steinem's achievements, in absolute terms, may not yet rank with those of outstanding women such as Golda Meir, Florence Nightingale, Margaret Sanger or Eleanor Roosevelt; however, her contribution to the liberation of women has been considerable. In addition, we should keep in mind that Ms. Gloria Steinem is still relatively young, and her career is still on the rise. Given her particular talents and the prospects of the rapid pace of events in modern times she might well become more than just a footnote in American history.

A CURRENT BIBLIOGRAPHY

There have been no full-length works written about Ms. Steinem. Listed below are some articles which are interesting and informative. The first series provides articles about her and the second the titles of some articles of interest that she has written.

Articles About Gloria Steinem

"Gloria Steinem," *Newsweek* (August 16, 1971), 51–54.

Mercer, M. "Woman of the Year," *McCall's* (January 1972), 67–69.

"Gloria in Excelsis. It's the Steinem Look," *Life* (August 11, 1972), 66–67.

Buckley, William F., Jr. "Ms. Davis and Steinem," *National Review* (December 31, 1971), 1486.

Levitt, L. "She," *Esquire* (October 1971), 87–89.

A Sampling of Articles Written by Gloria Steinem

"What We're All About," *Mental Hygiene* (Winter 1973), 14–16.

Smith, Liz. "Gloria Steinem, Writer and Social Critic, Talks About Sex, Politics and Marriage," *Redbook* (January, 1972), 69–76.

"Why We Need a Woman President in 1976," *Look* (January 13, 1970), 58.

"Woman for All Seasons," *McCalls* (May, 1967), 86–87.

Obtain back issues of *New York* and *Ms* magazine if you wish additional articles written by Ms. Steinem.

CHAPTER X

Billie Jean King

"... women show a front of iron"
Thomas Dunn English

In September, 1973, the Battle of the Sexes took on new dimensions as two giants of the nets took to the court at the Houston Astrodome before the largest crowd ever to attend a tennis match. In addition to the 30,742 people who watched the match live, there were an estimated forty-eight million television viewers. Pitted against each other in what was probably the most highly touted tennis match in history were fifty-five year old former tennis great Bobby Riggs, fresh from his Mother's Day victory over Mrs. Margaret Smith Court, and twenty-nine year old Billie Jean King, the reigning women's tennis star in the country. Using his carefully honed touch for the public relations bonanza, Bobby Riggs goaded and promoted a match between himself and Billie Jean King as the tennis match of the century. In many respects it was just that for the match drew reams of publicity, elicited enormous sums of money from various promotional devices, brought to the surface the simmering tensions between men and women and provided distraction for a nation beset by internal political and economic problems as well as international crises. The support for each player was divided along sexual lines. No one could predict the outcome with complete certainty. Within minutes after the match had begun the outcome was no longer in doubt. The old canard about women always being the weaker or the inferior sex was laid to rest as the result of Billie Jean King's annihilation of the "male superior" tennis game of Bobby Riggs.

NEW YORK SETS WORLD TEAM TENNIS

Billie Jean King

The hoopla that surrounded the match was capped by the entrance of the two players. Billie Jean King was borne onto the court on a red draped divan by four bare chested men wearing slave armbands while Bobby Riggs appeared in a rickshaw pulled by five beautiful girls. He presented her with a giant

Sugar Daddy "for the biggest sucker in the world," while she in turn gave him a live pig with the pointed name the Larimose Hustle. That was the end of the hoopla and the humor.

This eagerly awaited tennis match turned out to be the mismatch of the century. Billie Jean King blasted Bobby Riggs off the court in three straight sets with an overpowering display of greater stamina and superior play. Billie Jean drove him out of position repeatedly, fired low volleys at his feet, positioned him along the basepaths, and destroyed his famous lobs. Her deft position shots and backhand smashes and volleys drove him to his knees, and by the end of the match, all that Bobby Riggs was able to retain was enough energy to leap over the net to congratulate Billie Jean. The execution took but two hours and fifteen minutes. Billie Jean had helped to destroy the myth of male invincibility, and though Bobby Riggs retained his aplomb he lost the $100,000 purse in the winner take all stake arrangement for the match. In the relatively short span of several years Mrs. King had risen to the top of her profession and had become one of the most famous woman athletes in history. How she rose to those heights is a story of extraordinary discipline, remarkable commitment and almost obsessive singlemindedness.

Billie Jean Moffitt was born on November 22, 1943 in Long Beach, California, the daughter of a thirty-one year veteran of the Long Beach Fire Department. She was a tomboy in her early years, always in the middle of the rough and tumble games. An excellent all around athlete, she engaged in sports such as basketball, track and baseball. As a runner she outshone all the boys, and in the sixth grade she was the fastest runner in her elementary school. Billie Jean was never interested in dolls, sewing, or cooking, but rather in outdoor activities and sports. She played football, on one occasion winning the game by kicking a sixty yard field goal. As a member of the girl's basketball team at school she scored forty to fifty points a game.

Until she was eleven years of age Billie Jean knew nothing about tennis; however, her mother became concerned about her daughter's lack of femininity and insisted she choose from among swimming, tennis, or golf. This decision was arrived at shortly after her eleventh birthday. One evening, after playing a game of tennis with a friend, an excited and breathless Billie Jean Moffitt came home to announce that she was going to become a tennis player—the best woman tennis player in the world. Her father had bought her an eight dollar purple tennis racket, one with a velvet grip. She said she would be a winner at Wimbledon and six years later Billie Jean Moffitt became the youngest doubles champion at Wimbledon, one of the great tennis clubs in England and the world. From that triumph she went on to win six Wimbledon singles championships, the last in July, 1975, and three U.S. national singles titles and, in the process, was acknowledged as the greatest women's tennis player in the world. Her resounding victory over Bobby Riggs was the most widely publicized and viewed tennis match in history.

Mr. and Mrs. Moffitt, Billie Jean's parents, were instrumental in her success. Billie Jean was first trained by a tennis instructor at the Long Beach municipal parks. Mrs. Moffitt drove her daughter to a different public park every day for her tennis games. Here she learned the powerful, aggressive game that revolutionized women's tennis. Highly motivated and driven by her vision, Billie Jean would practice for four hours after school each night. Both mother and daughter shared a vision of greatness and accomplishment, so Mrs. Moffitt uncomplainingly drove her to tennis practice and sat alone hundreds and thousands of times watching her daughter going through her grueling regimen of practice and more practice. Sometimes she watched Billie Jean's brother, Randy, who had baseball practice. (Randy Moffitt is today a star baseball player with the San Francisco Giants.) On Saturdays Billie Jean practiced from early morning until darkness fell while her mother stood by loyally waiting to take her home. Mrs. Moffitt's support took other forms as well. To supplement the family's modest income and to provide finances for the equipment needs necessary to support her daughter's tennis ambitions, Mrs. Moffitt worked nights in a plastics factory. The future tennis star's almost superhuman drive was also illustrated by her desire to play the piano. In an effort to maintain both interests, Billie Jean practiced the piano for thirty minutes dressed in her tennis outfit. She then dashed off to the park for her tennis sessions.

Her thorough preparation coupled with great natural gifts soon began to bring returns for Billie Jean Moffitt. She captured her first trophy at the age of twelve, winning a Class D women's tournament in Long Beach. That award was the first of an avalanche of trophies that soon could be numbered in the dozens which she picked up during her years on the amateur tennis tournament circuits. Her high class qualities shone through even when she lost. Rather than sulking or emotionalizing, Billie Jean would analyze, practice and correct so that even her errors and losses were turned to her advantage.

Despite her almost all-consuming passion for tennis, Billie Jean managed during her high school years to follow at least the outward appearance of a normal teenager's life. She was a good student, went out on occasional dates and participated in some high school extra-curricular activities. In the main though, she pursued her dream of achieving tennis excellence. She rarely watched television or went to the movies and went to bed relatively early since she had to use her time and energy to further her dream of becoming a tennis champion. When she was sixteen she took lessons from Alice Marble, the great woman tennis star. Miss Marble worked with her for six months and was impressed by the teenager's talent and drive.

Religion played an important part in Billie Jean's life during those formative years. The Reverend Bob Richards, a former pole-vault Olympic champion was the pastor of the First Church of the Brethren, a few blocks from the Moffitt family's home. Reverend Richards baptized Billie Jean and imbued her with a religious spirit and also with a heightened awareness of the need for careful physical body conditioning.

In her senior year in high school Billie Jean walked three miles back and forth to school to strengthen her legs so that she could function better on the tennis court. Her awareness of the importance of tough physical training spurred her on during those walks as did her knowledge that she had to adopt a game strategy that was a departure from the usual tennis game women played. She began to play the net since she felt this was at the heart of men's superiority over women in tennis. Her critics notwithstanding, she stuck to her guns and played the net much to the regret of her hapless opponents who fell before her aggressive, driving, unusual game for a woman.

Billie Jean Moffitt was graduated from high school at the age of seventeen, but she did not even stay around Long Beach long enough to attend graduation exercises, leaving instead for Wimbledon. Once there she won the women's doubles competition with Karen Hantze. Billie Jean had no regrets about missing her high school graduation. Not only had she realized the dream she had nurtured since the age of twelve, but her coach, Clyde Walker, was in the terminal stages of cancer, and he survived long enough to learn of his star pupil's triumph.

Following the Wimbledon victory Billie Jean returned to California and entered Los Angeles State College, a school that she had selected in part because it was in the process of forming a women's tennis team. During her first two years at the college she lived at home, commuting by automobile from her home to college to save money. In 1962 Billie Jean returned to Wimbledon and achieved international fame with a stunning upset victory over Margaret Smith of Australia in the first round of the All-England championship. Miss Smith was at that time considered the greatest women's tennis player in the world and had been seeded first in the Wimbledon tournament.

Billie Jean returned to college and met Larry King, a pre-law student and soon she began dating him regularly. She and Larry were married on September 17, 1967, but their marriage (and even their courtship) was marked by tremendous pressures and long separations. Billie Jean continued to participate in a variety of amateur tournaments that took her all over the country, worked hard at tennis practice to maintain her form, and taught tennis in order to contribute to the young couple's financial support. Larry also worked in an ice cream container plant to help make ends meet.

Midway through her senior year at college Billie Jean decided to drop out of school much to the regret of her parents. Their daughter felt, however, that the demands of her tennis career and the responsibilities of marriage made it impossible for her to concentrate on school as well. Larry King was graduated from college in 1968 and enrolled in the law school of the University of California at Berkeley. Billie Jean helped him get through law school with "expense money" and "under the table" fees that she earned on the amateur tennis trail.

In 1967 Mrs. King became ill from typhus and was forced to take a leave from her rigorous tennis schedule. Ironically, that prolonged illness provided Billie Jean and Larry with the only year in their ten year marriage that they were not separated for long periods of time. Despite the long layoff Billie Jean retained her ranking as the number one American women's tennis player. In addition she was selected as the world's leading women's amateur tennis player in a poll of international sports writers. That year she was already being ranked near the top of the great women players in history.

1968 marked a historical high point for women's tennis. A world tennis tour for women was organized and Billie Jean and Larry faced their moment of truth. They recognized that once she joined the pro tour their lives would be irrevocably changed. Billie Jean and Larry weighed the alternatives and they agreed that she had to join the tour. She was immensely talented, tremendously interested and potentially great; she was also attracted to the money, excitement and glamor of the professional sports world. Billie Jean King signed her first professional tennis contract for $45,000 per year, a relatively modest sum by to-

day's tennis star standards. It was to be the beginning of a tremendously lucrative career.

That tour took Billie Jean to the "four corners of the earth"
while Larry remained behind to complete his law studies. They
kept in touch by mail and long-distance telephone but it was a
lonely, exacting life for the young couple.

Larry was graduated from law school and shortly thereafter
he passed the Hawaii bar examination. He then joined a Honolulu law firm where he practiced for some two years after which
he served as a sergeant in the United States Army Reserve for
six months. All this time he was also trying to manage his wife's
legal affairs to the best of his ability.

As Billie Jean King became increasingly successful, she went
on to win in all fourteen world titles and fifty-two national
championships from eleven nations, and her affairs became that
much more complex and demanding. By the end of 1970, three
years after their marriage her business affairs became so involved
that Larry left their home in Honolulu to return to Berkeley to
work with Tennis America, a corporation of which Billie Jean
was the chief officer. Larry King felt no inhibitions nor was he
plagued by any sense of inferiority though his wife was far more
successful than he. He accepted his role with complete equanimity.

In 1970 Billie Jean and Larry King faced a serious moral
issue. Billie Jean found herself pregnant. They had to examine
their lives once again and to arrive at an agonizing decision. If
she was to give birth to the child, Billie Jean would have to
abandon her tennis career while she was in her prime without
any guarantee that a layoff of a year more would not have a
seriously adverse effect on her game. On the other hand, abortion
was a step that raised significant moral, religious and medical
issues. They both agreed that an abortion would be best for
them since their lives were such that it would be unfair to bring
a child into the world. They were often apart—Billie Jean com-
peting in one city while Larry was engaged in promoting new

tournaments or working up contracts in another city. That decision was not made lightly, and it came back to haunt them in 1972 when Billie Jean joined fifty-three prominent women who signed an ad that later appeared in *Ms.* magazine attesting to their all having undergone abortions and urging the repeal of all anti-abortion laws. Her frank and outspoken views lost her many supporters.

The marriage of Billie Jean and Larry King is by no means an ordinary one. They are separated as much as forty weeks a year while she is on tennis tour and he practices law and looks after their affairs in Berkeley. Male ego notwithstanding, Larry is willing to remain a satellite to Billie Jean, the tennis celebrity and star. He is the manager and the prime mover though, serving in a variety of roles for her as agent, manager, lawyer, counselor, and companion. As vice president of World Team Tennis, a new professional tennis league, and board member of Tennis America, of which Billie Jean is president, he wields tremendous power over a network of fifteen tennis camps, grossing over two million dollars, tennis shops, sports figures, and a new sports magazine for women, *WomenSports*. She is the first woman athlete whose earnings have exceeded $100,000 in a single year. She recently signed a five year contract at more than $100,000 per year to be player coach of the Philadelphia entry in the World Tennis League. The Kings have helped make women's tennis big business on a par with all professional sports. In 1973 women shared equal purses with men at the U.S. Open Tennis Tournaments.

The effects of these long separations and the pressures of role reversals upon the marriage of Billie Jean and Larry King appear to be minimal. Both feel that despite the great amount of time they spend apart the time they do spend together more than makes up for the absences. They are also secure enough in their relationship to remain comfortable with each other in the face of the strains that their life style has placed upon them. Billie Jean is an adherent of the Women's Liberation movement in her feeling that women have every right to be fulfilled in whatever way suits them best, free of the restrictions of particular stereotyped roles assigned to women in our culture.

The Kings' frenzied pace has left them little time for the usual domestic life. Their house is almost a way station for them; they rarely eat there or spend a quiet evening at home. Yet they enjoy their life because they are doing what they like and what they feel is fulfilling.

For Billie Jean it has certainly been a life of achievement in the professional sense. The victory over Bobby Riggs was the capstone on a tennis career that has almost become a legend during the course of her own lifetime. The winner of dozens of tennis titles and championships, among them nine Wimbledon victories which include six Wimbledon titles which are particularly precious to her because of her childhood dream, she has also become the foremost spokeswoman in the country for women's tennis and women's sports. As a member of the President's Council on Physical Fitness and Sports and publisher of the new magazine, *WomenSports,* she continues to exercise a considerable amount of influence in the sports life of this country, a responsibility that she does not assume or discharge lightly.

Undisputed as the top women's ranking tennis player in the world, subject to displays of temperament on the court and driven by consuming energy and ambition, Billie Jean King has blazed new trails for women tennis players as well as all professional women athletes. She has achieved great fame as an athlete, amassed a considerable fortune from her tennis earnings and also has driven herself almost beyond the point of human endurance. Her accomplishments and her ability are unquestioned. One can only wonder how long she can maintain her grueling pace without jeopardizing her marriage through the pressures of her demanding professional life. Whatever the answer, what is clear is that Billie Jean King has established herself as one of the greatest women sports stars in the history of the world. Her achievements are a tribute to enormous drive, tremendous dedication, great skill and a loving and highly supportive family. She is also living proof of the power of an ideal and the force of a dream.

A CURRENT BIBLIOGRAPHY

King, Billie Jean with Kim Chapin. *Tennis to Win.* New York, Evanston and London: Harper and Row, 1970.

Olsen, James T. *Billie Jean King: Superstars.* New York: Creative Edition Books, 1974.

Consult the *Readers' Guide to Periodical Literature* for many current articles about Mrs. King.

King, Billie Jean with Kim Chapin. *Billie Jean.* New York, Evanston and London: Harper and Row, 1974.

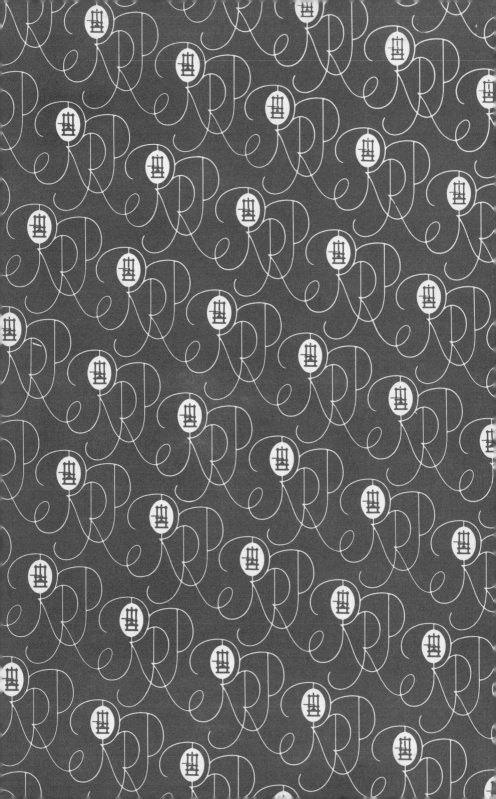